"Vicksburg National Military Park is one of the most densely monumented battlefields in the world, boasting of more than 1,300 pieces of commemorative art. The monuments of stone and bronze that dot the park landscape were executed by the foremost American sculptors of the late nineteenth and early twentieth centuries and have collectively made Vicksburg the 'art park of the world.' Michael Panhorst has produced for the first time the story of those sculptures—their design, symbolism, and meaning. It is a story as rich and compelling as the monuments themselves."

—Terrence J. Winschel, Historian (ret.),
Vicksburg National Military Park

"Panhorst's volume singlehandedly redresses a longtime lacuna in American sculpture scholarship by giving a colorful voice to the artistic and cultural significance of commemorative memorials created in the South during the post–Civil War decades. It appeals not only as a fascinating take-along guidebook at Vicksburg but also as a readily comprehensible primer on the processes and materials of monument-making, certain to appeal to scholars and lay enthusiasts of sculpture, architecture, historic preservation, and Civil War studies alike."

—Thayer Tolles, Marica F. Vilcek Curator of American
Paintings and Sculpture, The Metropolitan Museum of Art

"Michael Panhorst's book is more than a compendium of Vicksburg's commemorative works in bronze and stone. Through a series of short essays, he invites readers to see monument-making as the product of many hands and minds. Veterans, politicians, sculptors, architects, foundry workers, and stonecutters all had roles to play. In more recent years, we have added to the mix the conservators and maintenance staffs who care for these treasures. Complementing this comprehensive work is a richly illustrated driving tour that is sure to inspire Vicksburg's visitors to get out of their cars and take a closer look."

—Dennis Montagna, Ph.D., Historian and monument
preservation manager

Spirit of the Republic, Missouri Monument, Victor Holm, 1917

THE
MEMORIAL
ART AND
ARCHITECTURE
OF

Vicksburg
National
Military
Park

THE KENT STATE
UNIVERSITY PRESS
KENT, OHIO

Michael W. Panhorst

All photos are by the author unless otherwise noted.
All maps are by Erin Greb Cartography.

Library of Congress Catalog Card Number 2014015055
ISBN 978-1-60635-219-9
Manufactured in China

Library of Congress Cataloging-in-Publication Data

Panhorst, Michael W.
  The memorial art and architecture of Vicksburg National Military Park /
Michael W. Panhorst.
      pages cm
   Includes bibliographical references.
ISBN 978-1-60635-219-9 (hardcover) ∞
1. Vicksburg National Military Park (Miss.)—Guidebooks.
2. War memorials—Mississippi—Vicksburg National Military Park—Guidebooks.
3. Monuments—Mississippi—Vicksburg National Military Park—Guidebooks.
4. Sculpture—Mississippi—Vicksburg National Military Park—Guidebooks.
5. Architecture—Mississippi—Vicksburg National Military Park—Guidebooks.
I. Title.
  E475.27.P36 2014
  973.7'344—dc23
                        2014015055

19 18 17 16 15   5 4 3 2 1

Contents

Foreword

Edwin C. Bearss

My first awareness of memorial art was associated with Lt. Col. George Armstrong Custer. It surfaced because I grew up on a cattle ranch in Big Horn Country in Montana. The family ranch was within 30 miles, as the crow flies, of what was then designated the National Cemetery of Custer's Battlefield Reservation and is now the Little Bighorn Battlefield National Monument. Prior to my 1942 enlistment in the U.S. Marine Corps, I had visited that hallowed ground twice. Then there was only one truncated obelisk on the field known as "Last Stand Hill." It marks the mass grave where most of the enlisted men who rode with Custer are buried. There was another memorial that I passed each school day I attended second, third, and fourth grades in Hardin, Montana. It was located in Custer Memorial Park, and it featured a bronze medallion of Custer's face in profile affixed to a granite block.

It was only when I was a graduate student at Indiana University in July 1954 that I experienced an epiphany and recognized the significance of battlefield memorial art. I did my Master's thesis on Maj. Gen. Patrick R. Cleburne, the "Stonewall Jackson of the West." After completing my thesis, but before submitting it, I determined to visit the battlefields where Cleburne and his command fought. Among these were four administered by the National Park Service (NPS). Shiloh National Military Park and Chickamauga and Chattanooga National Military Park each featured many memorials. The other two, Kennesaw Mountain National Battlefield Park and Stones River National Battlefield, had only a few.

At Shiloh I met Park Historian Charles E. "Pete" Shedd, who took me in hand. We visited the site of the oak tree (no longer standing) where Governor Isham Harris discovered the mortally wounded Albert Sidney Johnston, and we walked into the ravine where Johnston died. We stopped at the Confederate Monument erected by the United Daughters of the Confederacy and dedicated in May 1917. I left Shiloh that day with a better appreciation of memorial art and its educational value.

Within fourteen months, on September 28, 1956, my dream to become a park historian at Vicksburg National Military Park (VNMP) came true. But when I joined the NPS family, I had never been to Vicksburg. Besides having to familiarize myself with the ebb and flow of the battle and campaign, I was confronted by a major challenge: to learn as much as possible about the battlefield park's magnificent collection of memorial art—its whereabouts, significance, and associated trivia. Park staffers—particularly several who had been associated with VNMP for more than two decades—and the park's files got me off to a jump start. But it was several months before I got to the point where I could entertain and enlighten park visitors. Thus, early in my 41-year NPS career, I came to appreciate the importance of Civil War memorial art.

Near the other end of my NPS career, when I served as Chief Historian of the NPS, I was introduced to Michael Panhorst by two of my NPS colleagues: Chief Historical Architect Hugh Miller and Susan Sherwood, who managed an NPS program focusing on the adverse impact of acid rain on outdoor memorial art and other cultural resources. Like Miller and Sherwood, I was impressed with Panhorst's credentials and interests. This led to our endorsement that encouraged Eastern National Park and Monument Association (now Eastern National) to support Panhorst's research on Civil War battlefield monuments with financial support.

I only wish that Michael had published *The Memorial Art and Architecture of Vicksburg National Military Park* in the mid-1950s. It would have made my task easier and abbreviated my learning curve!

Preface

This book is more about memorial art and architecture than it is about the arts of war. It is less about the Civil War era than it is about the era of sectional reconciliation and national reunification around the fortieth and fiftieth anniversaries of the war when Civil War veterans and their families and friends memorialized the men and events of the war then rapidly receding into history. Between the time when sons of Union and Confederate veterans (and a few Civil War veterans themselves) fought side by side in Cuba and the Philippines in the Spanish-American War in 1898 and the time when those soldiers and their sons and daughters went "over there" to fight "The War to End All Wars" in 1917, America's battlefields at Gettysburg, Antietam, Shiloh, Chickamauga and Chattanooga, and Vicksburg were transformed from private farms and forests into national military parks marked with monuments and memorials to the men and events of the Civil War. This book is about how the collective memory of a grateful nation and the creative arts of sculpture and architecture transformed Vicksburg into the commemorative art park of the South.

Acknowledgments

This book began its gestation about 1983, when Wayne Craven, my dissertation advisor in the department of art history at the University of Delaware, suggested that I explore the memorial art and architecture at Vicksburg National Military Park because the park needed a book similar to his *The Sculptures at Gettysburg* (1982). With the guidance of Professor Craven and his faculty colleagues Damie Stillman, William Homer, and Roberta Tarbell, I wrote my dissertation about the monuments and memorial sculptures in national military parks on Civil War battlefields at Vicksburg, Gettysburg, Shiloh, Antietam, and Chickamauga and Chattanooga. George Gurney, a University of Delaware Ph.D. and then curator of sculpture at the Smithsonian's National Museum of American Art, was my advisor for a Smithsonian predoctoral fellowship.

Eastern National Park and Monument Association supported my work with a grant that proved to be the precursor to the Ronald F. Lee Fellowship, and the National Park Service's Washington office provided access to the recently computerized List of Classified Structures. Ed Bearss, Hugh Miller, and Susan Sherwood, all in the Washington office, encouraged my research, and Sherwood provided vital financial support through related acid rain research contracts funded by the National Acid Precipitation Assessment Program.

Over the years, National Park Service historians, librarians, archivists, and rangers have helped me get both the big picture and the minute details regarding Civil War battlefield monuments, but special thanks for assistance with this book are due to Terry Winschel and Elizabeth Joyner at VNMP.

Bill Seratt, director of the Vicksburg Convention and Visitors Bureau, also helped by asking me to write and illustrate a lengthy brochure on this topic. That publication was ultimately tabled, but the project facilitated much of this writing and many of the photographs.

Three great friends who share my passion for outdoor sculptures and public monuments and their preservation also deserve mention here. Cameron Wilson, Tom Podnar, and Dennis Montagna have all sustained and supported me at various times. I hope they can share in the satisfaction of seeing this in print.

I am eternally grateful to those mentioned above, and to those un-named who have helped over the years. I am especially grateful to my family for their patience and encouragement.

1 Introduction to Vicksburg National Military Park

President Abraham Lincoln called Vicksburg "the key" and believed that the war would not be won by the Union until that key was "in our pocket." As the Civil War wore into its second and third years, Union efforts focused on capturing the heavily fortified citadel on the Mississippi River that prevented the Father of Waters from flowing, as Lincoln said, "unvexed to the sea" (fig. 1.1).

In May of 1863, Gen. Ulysses S. Grant and about 45,000 soldiers—most from the Midwest—laid siege to the city and about 50,000 Confederate soldiers—most from the Deep South. After 47 days and combined casualties of 20,000, Gen. John C. Pemberton surrendered the city—on the same day that Gen. Robert E. Lee began his retreat from the Confederate defeat at Gettysburg. The war lasted another two years, but the Confederacy never surpassed its high-water mark on Cemetery Ridge at Gettysburg, and it never regained control of Vicksburg and the Mississippi River.

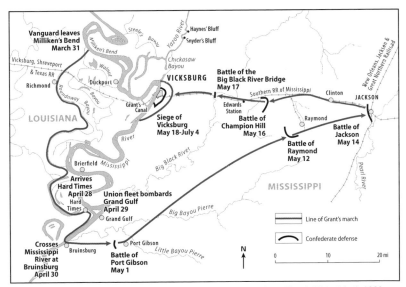

Fig. 1.1. Vicksburg Campaign Map showing Grant's movements from March 31 to July 4, 1863

In the decade after Appomattox, survivors of the war—North and South—focused on healing their war wounds. The bodies of Union dead were systematically collected from shallow battlefield graves and re-interred in new national cemeteries like Vicksburg National Cemetery, the largest in the country with 17,000 burials. With no Confederate government to organize and fund reburial and commemoration of its fallen defenders, the Confederate dead were dependent on the charity of a defeated, demoralized, and economically devastated people. Consequently, white Southern women assumed responsibility for reburying the Confederate dead and raising monuments to their memory like that in Cedar Hill Cemetery (fig. 2.1).

By the twenty-fifth anniversary of the war, veterans had begun to raise markers and memorials along Union lines at Gettysburg that had been protected by a private preservation group. In the 1890s, battlefield preservation advocates established national military parks at Gettysburg (1895), Antietam (1890), Shiloh (1894), Chickamauga and Chattanooga (1890), and Vicksburg (1899). During the period of economic prosperity and national expansion between the World's Columbian Exposition in Chicago in 1893 and the U.S. entry into World War I in 1917, the states vied once again on Civil War battlefields, but this time the contest was about which state would honor its volunteer soldiers in the most effective manner.

At Vicksburg, Northern states led the way with impressive structures commemorating all the soldiers from their states who served at Vicksburg. Illinois (figs. 5.2, 5.3, 5.4) built a memorial resembling the ancient Roman Pantheon. Iowa constructed an elaborate exedra, an ancient Roman monument form shaped like a bench or seat, and ornamented it with an equestrian color bearer and six bronze relief sculptures depicting scenes from the campaign and siege (fig. 3.3). Most Northern state memorials were in place by World War I, but many Southern state memorials were not placed until the centennial of the war or later because of less abundant financial resources and a reluctance to mark a battlefield where the South had lost.

In 1903, Massachusetts became the first state to dedicate a monument—a heroic-scale bronze *Volunteer* (fig. 11.5) marching to war. The sculptor, Theo Alice Ruggles Kitson, was a native of Massachusetts and one of only three female members of the National Sculpture Society. Her mentor and husband, sculptor Henry Kitson, supervised placement of the memorial because she was home with their infant daughter, but she returned the favor a few years later when she made most of the equestrian color bearer for Henry's *Iowa Monument* while he was ill. In addition to the Massachusetts and Iowa memorials, the Kitsons created 3 portrait figures, 24 portrait busts, and 54 portrait reliefs—many more than any of the other sculptors represented at Vicksburg.

Fig. 1.2. *General Stevenson* and the old VNMP Administration Building near the site of the *Surrender Interview Marker*

The predominance of portrait memorials at Vicksburg results from the commemorative program orchestrated by the park commission that supervised the creation and operation of the park under the War Department until 1933, when responsibility for national military parks was transferred to the National Park Service. William T. Rigby, a Vicksburg veteran from Iowa who served as the resident commissioner from 1901 to 1928, effectively promoted the program of portraying each commander of a battery or brigade or larger group of soldiers. A total of 177 portrait figures, busts, and reliefs (fig. 1.2) line the park roads traversed each year by hundreds of thousands of visitors. The portraits, allegorical sculptures, and architectural monuments mark the battlefield and memorialize the men and events of the campaign and siege. They tell the history of the epic battle as well as the story of its survivors, who commemorated their comrades, fathers, sons, and brothers in imperishable granite and bronze.

2 : Overview of Memorial Art and Architecture at Vicksburg

This book surveys the memorial art and architecture found in and around Vicksburg National Military Park (VNMP). The park preserves the battle lines encircling the northern and eastern perimeter of the Civil War–era city, plus a few outlying monuments and memorials dedicated to the

Fig. 2.1. *Monument to the Confederate Dead,* Cedar Hill Cemetery

1862–63 campaign, siege, and eventual surrender of the Gibraltar of the Confederacy. During the heyday of commemorative efforts shortly after 1900, many local park boosters and countless park visitors recognized the effect of these memorials on the historic landscape. It was called the "Art Park of the South."

The subject of most of this commemorative art is the courage and selfless devotion to duty of the 100,000 soldiers and sailors from 29 states who fought for months to control Vicksburg and the Mississippi River. The service and sacrifice of these men, approximately 20,000 of whom were killed, wounded, or went missing, was recognized during and immediately after the war with monuments in cemeteries and on courthouse lawns around the country like Vicksburg's *Monument to the Confederate Dead* (fig. 2.1). Few monuments were erected at Vicksburg or other Civil War battlefields until decades passed and survivors gained historical distance from the horrific and heroic events of the war.

By the 1890s, veterans realized that the sites of their martial exploits were being lost—in some cases to land development and in others to neglect. A movement began in earnest to protect and preserve important battlefields and to mark them with durable memorials. Union and Confederate veterans in Congress led efforts to appropriate funds to establish national military parks administered by the War Department at Vicksburg (1899), Gettysburg (1895), Shiloh (1894), Antietam (1890), and Chickamauga and Chattanooga (1890). As the fortieth and fiftieth anniversaries of the battles passed, aging warriors returned to the fields to pay homage to their fallen comrades, to their brothers in arms, and to their adversaries, whose courage and military prowess they respected. They journeyed back to Vicksburg and other battlefields to dedicate monuments and to commemorate the men and events of the war "without praise and without censure," as national military park regulations required.

Many veterans participated in joint reunion encampments of Blue and Gray that became popular on the preserved battlefields. Those events not only reflected the reconciliation then occurring between North and South, they also facilitated it. And, as might be expected, the growing spirit of reconciliation and national reunification was memorialized in battlefield monuments like the *Missouri Monument* with its *Spirit of the Republic* (cover, frontispiece, fig. 2.2), a winged *Nike* or victory figure that wears a Phrygian bonnet like ancient Roman freed slaves, and carries a fasces, a bundle of rods symbolic of strength through unity, as well as an olive branch, which is emblematic of peace.

The commemorative spirit of Civil War survivors and their families takes a variety of forms ranging from compact gravestones for the unknown dead to large memorials like the Missouri, Illinois (figs. 5.2, 5.3, 5.4), and Iowa (fig. 3.3) monuments, which are dedicated to all of the troops from an individual state. At Vicksburg, commanders of batteries, brigades, divisions, corps, and armies are depicted in reliefs and busts, as well as many full-length statues, including three equestrian portraits.

Patrons' penchants for realism dictated that these effigies of specific individuals represent them accurately, especially in terms of physical appearance, uniforms, and equipment. Generic images of common soldiers such as those on the Wisconsin (fig. 3.4) and Mississippi (Driving Tour [DT]57) monuments were also expected to be anatomically correct and authentically equipped. Statues personifying Michigan (DT7, DT8), History (DT57), Peace (fig. 6.1), and other ideas are appropriately more generalized in appearance. Most of these allegorical figures are cloaked in voluminous gowns or flowing drapery suggestive of ancient Greek and Roman statuary, which was widely admired during the City Beautiful movement (1893–1917), when classical revival styles dominated public art and architecture and when most Civil War battlefield monuments were dedicated.

The story of these sculptural and architectural forms, their patronage, design, production, placement, and meaning illuminate the memorial art and architecture at Vicksburg, the commemorative art park of the South.

Fig. 2.2. *Nike, Missouri Monument*

3 The Art Park of the South

Most of the memorials in VNMP were placed there during the two decades following establishment of the park by act of Congress in 1899. By the time the United States entered World War I in 1917 and popular interest shifted to soldiers of that war, hundreds of monuments and markers had been erected to memorialize the siege and defense of Vicksburg. Most of the monuments on the field today commemorate those who served at Vicksburg, but some, like the equestrian portrait of Gen. Lloyd Tilghman (fig. 3.1), who was killed at Champion Hill on May 16, 1863, recognize the service of soldiers who fell in the months of campaigning that culminated in the May 18–July 4 siege. A few memorials are dedicated to Gen. Joseph Johnston's nearby Confederate Army of Relief, which had failed to aid Vicksburg's defenders.

Around the turn of the twentieth century, Civil War battlefields at Gettysburg, Shiloh, Antietam, Chickamauga and Chattanooga, and a

Fig. 3.1. *Gen. Lloyd Tilghman Monument*

few other sites were marked in a similar fashion. Gettysburg and Chicka-mauga and Chattanooga accumulated collections of memorial art and architecture as large as that at Vicksburg. Vicksburg's commemorative structures, however—which currently total about 1,350 monuments, memorials, and markers—appear more concentrated physically and more consistent stylistically than the memorials at Gettysburg, Shiloh, Antietam, and Chickamauga and Chattanooga for several reasons.

The physical concentration results from the application of War Depart-ment rules governing the placement of markers and memorials, plus the topographic realities of the siege. At each of the national military parks, regulations generally restricted placement of memorials for regiments and batteries to documented positions of the units in the line of battle, while permitting brigade, division, and state memorials to be placed in prominent positions that had been occupied by those troops. Because the Vicksburg campaign culminated in a classic siege operation, both armies were deeply entrenched. Their positions were clearly marked by remnants of earthworks that were discernable in 1899 and are visible today due to their restoration in the 1930s. Most troops manned the same section of the lines throughout the siege, although many of them, like Gen. Isham Garrott (fig. 3.2), who was shot by a Union sharpshooter, died on the ramparts. Consequently, state and regimental monuments to the troops, as well as statuary depicting the commanders, are concentrated along the relatively fixed line of battle at Vicksburg rather than being more widely distributed as they are on most other Civil War battlefields where troop movements were more fluid.

In addition to being concentrated along the siege lines, Vicksburg's monuments are also concentrated in terms of their dedication dates. Most were placed between the establishment of the national military park in 1899 and the U.S. entry into World War I in 1917. In contrast, the earliest memorials at Gettysburg date from right after the war, and many were erected in the 1880s around the twenty-fifth anniversary of the battle. Likewise, memorialization at Chickamauga and Chattanooga began with that sprawling park's establishment in 1890. As a result of the earlier com-memorative efforts at those parks, the memorial art and architecture there reflect a wider range of stylistic treatment than is found in the monuments at Vicksburg, which were designed and constructed according to the Beaux Arts aesthetics that dominated public art and architecture in the United States in the wake of the "White City" of the World's Columbian Exposition in Chicago in 1893 and up through the 1920s.

The neoclassical architectural style of the temporary "White City" popu-larized a nationwide taste for classical columns, pediments, and pedestals in monochromatic, light-toned stone—preferably marble, limestone, or granite—as exemplified in the *Iowa Monument* (fig. 3.3). Ancient monu-ment forms such as obelisks, triumphal arches, and exedra dominated the

Fig. 3.2. *Gen. Isham Garrott Monument*

designs of sculptors and architects, many of whom were trained in Paris at the École des Beaux-Arts or similar academies in Europe or the United States. Those designers created memorial architecture that was distinctly different in style and material from the heavily rusticated, polychromatic stone structures like the *New Hampshire Monument* (DT22) that had been popular earlier and that can be found in abundance at Gettysburg, and Chickamauga and Chattanooga. Moreover, in contrast to the rigidly realistic sculptural style popular in the Victorian era, the statuary that adorns most Beaux Arts monuments displays an invigorated naturalism that was influenced by contemporary French academic sculptors; that statuary was

Fig. 3.3. *Iowa Monument*

Fig. 3.4. *Infantry, Wisconsin Memorial*

integrated into the overall architectural designs more fully. This is especially evident in the Missouri, Michigan, and Wisconsin (fig. 3.4) monuments (discussed in more detail below), all of which were dedicated between 1911 and 1917.

Another distinguishing characteristic of the commemorative art and architecture at Vicksburg is the predominance of portrait memorials. Under the leadership of William Rigby (fig. 3.5), who chaired the VNMP commission from 1901 to 1928, the commission created a unique memorialization program utilizing portraits of every individual

Fig. 3.5. *VNMP Commissioner William T. Rigby*

who commanded a battery, brigade, or larger body of troops at Vicksburg. Three generals were commemorated with equestrian sculptures, and fourteen commanders (as well as Abraham Lincoln, Jefferson Davis, and Indiana's war governor Oliver Morton) were memorialized with full-length statues, most during the three decades of Rigby's park commission leadership. Sixty-three men were depicted in busts and ninety-four more were pictured in life-sized reliefs. Vicksburg is the only national military park on a Civil War battlefield with a commemorative program that preferred one monument form to another. The other national military parks accepted whatever monument designs were submitted for portraits (equestrian, pedestrian figure, bust, relief), shaft memorials (obelisks, columns, stelae, etc.), or exedra, as well as more eccentric compositions.

The concentration of monuments and memorial sculptures along the siege lines around Vicksburg, coupled with the consistent scale and materials of the Beaux Arts structures and the predominance of the portrait monument form, evoke the "art park" atmosphere. The park-like setting accentuates this as well. The dense woods that line many of the park roads today isolate visitors from the surrounding area and its post–Civil War development; however, some of the woods are themselves postwar intrusions on the historic battlefield. Over time, trees and brush reclaimed some of the barren landscapes that had been cleared by the Confederate army in the construction of its defensive works, and in the 1930s additional trees were planted to prevent erosion. Recent restoration efforts have reopened historic vistas like that between the Iowa and Texas monuments on the park's South Loop Road, and that between the Michigan and Louisiana monuments on the north loop (fig. 3.6). Still,

Civil War soldiers saw much more open ground and fewer trees than do modern visitors driving along the park's tour roads.

Those roads are also postwar intrusions on the historic battlefield. They were originally built as dirt and gravel tracks in the early twentieth century to facilitate battlefield tours. Consequently, they follow the terrain closely without altering it much. Those roads still utilize many of the century-old bridges that over time have also become historic structures.

Today the tour roads are lined with monuments and historic markers. Early in the twentieth century, red and blue cast-iron markers (fig. 3.7) were erected to document Confederate and Union troop positions and to interpret the battle for visitors. More than 140 were removed and sacrificed to the war effort in World War II, but 594 remain, and the park is working to replace some of those that are missing. There are also 70 bronze markers. Each of these 664 plaques was carefully worded and sited to communicate exactly what happened when and where on the historic field.

Decommissioned cannon were also commonly employed at Vicksburg and other national military parks to mark battery sites. Today, 141 Civil War cannon tubes mounted on twentieth-century cast-iron carriages

Fig. 3.6. Approach to the *Louisiana Monument*

Fig. 3.7. Cast-iron plaques tell of hand-to-hand combat at Railroad Redoubt

Fig. 3.8. Battery de Golyer

Fig. 3.9. *Gen. Daniel W. Adams Monument* with the colossal *Louisiana Monument* and a plaque in the distance

document the placement of many big guns during the battle (fig. 3.8), and they evoke the fearful firepower characteristic of Civil War engagements. Yet the extant cannon represent just a portion of the ordnance on the ground during the battle. An impressive array of cannon tubes near the Visitor Center illustrates the variety of bronze and cast-iron mortars, howitzers, naval, and field guns used during the war.

Interpretive displays such as the markers, monuments, roads, and trees have a visual impact on modern visitors to the battlefield, and that impact is not entirely positive. Postwar intrusions like the modern Visitor Center, parking lot, and maintenance and administration buildings help to protect, preserve, and interpret the campaign, siege, and defense of Vicksburg, but they can also get in the way of visitors appreciating the heroic events that occurred on this historic ground. Still, the steep grades and narrow gauge of the park roads lined with monuments, markers, and cannon create just the effect intended by the VNMP Commission (fig. 3.9)—a national park that preserves a historic site and commemorates the people who made it historic.

4 : Patronage of Memorial Art and Architecture at Vicksburg

Memorial art and architecture at Vicksburg and other Civil War battlefield parks was funded by federal and state governments, individual veterans, groups such as the Grand Army of the Republic and United Daughters of the Confederacy, and relatives of the veterans. Congress provided money for five specific purposes: 1) to purchase land; 2) to map the parks; 3) to locate troop positions; 4) to mark those positions with condemned ordnance, cast-iron tablets, and modest markers; and 5) to erect monuments to the U.S. Regular Army units that saw action on the battlefields. At Vicksburg, the federal government also funded the 202-foot-tall *U.S. Navy Memorial* (fig. 4.1). Because the vast majority of soldiers were volunteers who served in regiments raised by the various states, the states assumed primary responsibility for commemorating their troops. In general, Northern states acted more quickly and were more generous than Southern states, the economies of which had recovered from the war more slowly. Moreover, Confederate veterans were less eager to revisit the early national battlefield parks where, with the exception of Chickamauga, they had suffered defeat.

Upon creation of VNMP, most of the states that sent troops to Vicksburg (primarily Midwestern and Deep South states) appointed veterans of the campaign and siege to commissions that visited the field with park officials to locate and mark their positions. Then the states commissioned monuments and memorials. Like Iowa, most Northern states commissioned relatively modest monuments (fig. 4.2) to mark the position of batteries and regiments as well as more elaborate monuments to commemorate all of their soldiers in a single structure. Southern states tended to erect a single sizeable monument and few, if any, unit memorials, but Mississippi (fig. 4.3) was an exception. Some Southern states did not memorialize their troops at Vicksburg until the centennial of the war, or until much later in the case of Tennessee (1996) and Kentucky (2001). Connecticut (which had a single regiment at Vicksburg during the 1862 campaign, and no representation in 1863) did not erect a memorial at Vicksburg until just a few years before the war's sesquicentennial, by which time Congress had expanded the purview of the park to include the 1862 campaign.

Fig. 4.1. *U.S. Navy Memorial*

Since public funds were utilized and everyone wanted the finest memorial that limited money could buy, state commissions generally relied on competitions to select the designers and builders. Competitions varied from a few local companies submitting sealed bids for structures of a specific shape, size, or budget to competitions open to anyone able to submit drawings and/or models. Designs were often displayed in the state house for public comment, and some competitions required that designs be marked with a cipher to maintain the anonymity of the artist. Then as now, few competitions were totally "blind," and politics surely played a role in some selections. The most highly regarded sculptors and architects of the day despised such public competitions because of the politics, because their ideas might be pirated by others in future competitions, and because of the substantial investment of time and energy with little chance of success. Consequently, there are no sculptures by Augustus

Fig. 4.2. *Tenth and Seventeenth Iowa Monument*   Fig. 4.3. *Company A, Mississippi Light Artillery Monument*

Fig. 4.4. Detail of the head of *Gen. Stephen Dill Lee Monument*

Saint-Gaudens or Daniel Chester French—the greatest American sculptors active around 1900—at Vicksburg or the other battlefield parks. Statuary by very competent students and assistants of these and other master sculptors abounds, however. The magnificent state-funded equestrian portrait of Illinois's Gen. John McClernand (fig. 15.3) by Edward Potter, who assisted French by modeling the horses for the master sculptor's equestrian groups, is a case in point.

A good example of the patronage system at Vicksburg is the handsome bronze figure of Gen. Stephen Dill Lee (fig. 4.4) by Henry Hudson Kitson. Lee served as chairman of the VNMP commission from 1899 to 1901 and remained an active member until his death in 1908. He was the only Confederate veteran elected to chair a national military park commission. He also served as Commander-in-Chief of the United Confederate Veterans (1904–8) and as president of the college known today as Mississippi State University. Upon his death, his son and friends in 28 states (including President Theodore Roosevelt) contributed to his memorial. The VNMP commission used some of its federal appropriation to prepare the foundation for Lee's portrait and to supervise its placement, as it did with all memorial art and architecture at Vicksburg.

Fig. 4.5. *Gen. John Pemberton Monument*

Fig. 4.6. *Gen. Ulysses S. Grant Monument*

The VNMP commission also used part of its annual appropriation to buy and install pedestals for a few reliefs and busts funded by family and friends of the subjects. Moreover, by 1917 the federal government had fully funded seven statues, forty-nine busts, and fifty-nine reliefs—the vast majority of the statuary at Vicksburg. Over nearly three decades as resident commissioner and then chairman of the VNMP commission, William T. Rigby commissioned numerous portraits with federal funding through sealed bids from a short list of sculptors who had previously done good, timely, cost-effective work for the park. VNMP was the only national military park to employ this procurement practice.

Ironically, Edmond Quinn's statue of Gen. John Pemberton (fig. 4.5), the Confederate commander during the campaign and siege, was funded by the Federal government. Pemberton, a native of Pennsylvania, was virtually disowned by his home state for casting his lot with the Confederacy and was also out of favor in the postwar South because Southerners felt he should have saved the city. To assure adequate representation of this Confederate leader, the VNMP commission had no choice but to fund the portrait from its annual budget, an act that required approval from the secretary of war. The slightly larger than life-sized figure on its simple stone base is accurate enough, but it pales in comparison with Frederick Hibbard's heroic-scale equestrian portrait of Pemberton's adversary, Gen. Ulysses S. Grant, on its imposing pedestal flanked by two granite benches (fig. 4.6), an ensemble generously funded by the state of Illinois, the state where Grant lived immediately before and after the Civil War.

5 : Memorial Art and Architecture Design Process

Once funding was secured for Civil War battlefield monuments and memorials, design could commence. As discussed above, design competitions often determined the selection of sculptors and architects. Portrait reliefs, busts, and figures generally did not require the involvement of an architect or engineer, as did the larger structures. Sometimes, as with the *Iowa Monument* (fig. 3.3), a sculptor created the design and hired an architect to provide specifications and to supervise construction. In other cases, as with the *Wisconsin Monument,* an architect or engineer was the primary designer, and sculptors were subcontracted for statuary and ornament. For the *Wisconsin Monument,* the designer, Liance Cottrell, even provided drawings for sculptor Julius Loester to translate into the three-dimensional forms of the monumental infantry and cavalry figures (fig. 5.1) and the three bronze reliefs on the base of the colossal column.

Fig. 5.1. *Cavalry, Wisconsin Monument*

Fig. 5.2. *Illinois Memorial* and Shirley House

Fig. 5.3. *Illinois Memorial*   Fig. 5.4. *Illinois Memorial* pediment

The design of the largest and most expensive monument at Vicksburg—indeed, on any Civil War battlefield by 1917—the $195,000 *Illinois Memorial* (figs. 5.2, 5.3, 5.4), is generally credited to William LeBaron Jenney, a prominent Chicago architect and engineer, who pioneered skeletal steel-frame construction after the war. However, many people were actually involved in the design process. According to the official report of the Illinois–Vicksburg Military Park Commission, in 1903 the commission's Committee on Designs employed Jenney "to aid the committee" in the preparation of designs for the monuments and markers to be erected by the commission. After "almost daily consultation" with Jenney and others and "weeks of elaboration in the drafting rooms of Messrs. Jenney and Mundie, architects," commission chair Francis A. Riddle "conceived and presented" a design for the state monument.

Jenney had served as chief of General Sherman's engineers at Vicksburg, and he had been on the committee appointed by the governor in 1901 to locate the position of Illinois troops at Vicksburg. Thus his involvement in preliminary design decisions (for which the committee authorized payment of up to $200 upon approval of the design) does not seem unusual. However, this method of developing a monument design from within the commission while utilizing the aid of a hand-picked professional was not common.

Once the design was selected, Jenney's firm was retained to develop the design, execute the blueprints, and supervise construction of the structure. The architects subcontracted an independent sculptor to provide plaster models for the sculpture in the design and to supervise the execution of those models in Georgia marble. Charles Mulligan, sculpture instructor at the Art Institute of Chicago, was chosen to model the three-figure marble pedimental group of *History Recording the Deeds of North and South* (fig. 5.4) and three bust-length portraits located under the portico. Another Chicago sculptor, Frederick C. Hibbard, was employed to make the spread-winged bronze eagle that was cast by Chicago's American Bronze Company for the apex of the pediment.

6 Styles and Aesthetics of Memorial Art and Architecture at Vicksburg

The involvement of multiple designers, artists, and artisans in the design and production of individual memorials was typical during the early twentieth century, when American art and architecture were dominated by Beaux Arts aesthetics. Many of America's top architects had trained at the École des Beaux-Arts in Paris, and they in turn taught others to use a classical vocabulary of architectural forms (e.g., columns, cornices, and pediments) richly embellished with ornamental and symbolic sculpture. Beaux Arts sculptors made bold figurative statuary that was often enveloped in heavy draperies, the deep folds of which created a sharp contrast between dark shadows and brightly highlighted forms. William Couper's *Peace* (fig. 6.1), at the base of the heavily rusticated obelisk of the *Minnesota Monument,* is a good example of Beaux Arts statuary, but Beaux Arts architectural elements generally have smoother surfaces, like those of the *Wisconsin Monument.* Perhaps the best examples of Beaux Arts–style memorials at Vicksburg are the *Iowa Monument* (fig. 3.3) and *Missouri Monument* (DT42), both of which thoroughly integrate figurative sculpture with an exedra, one of the most popular Beaux Arts monument forms.

Beaux Arts aesthetics dominated American monument and memorial design until the Great Depression. In the 1930s and 1940s, Art Deco and Art Moderne styles favored more simplified and stylized architecture and sculpture, but those decades saw little commemorative art built at Vicksburg or other Civil War parks. After World War II, Modernist architects designed buildings like the VNMP Visitor Center (1970), with its flattened, planar forms and absence of applied ornament. In Modern architecture form follows function, but architects exploited contrasts in the color and texture of building materials such as brick, glass, steel, and stone.

The *Arkansas Monument,* dedicated in 1954, and the *Georgia Monument,* dedicated in 1962, are good examples of commemorative art in the Modern architectural style but they show traces of earlier Art Moderne, Art Deco, and Beaux Arts aesthetics. The *Arkansas Monument* (fig. 6.2) has an exedral form, but one severely simplified into flat, angular forms with hard edges and no moldings. Its pictorial relief sculpture is also flattened, angular, and stylized, like much representational sculpture of its day. The *Georgia Monument* (fig. 6.3) is devoid of sculpture except for a small state seal carved in the tall shaft. The monument is rigidly architectonic, rather like a 1950s Art Moderne skyscraper, complete with fluted panels on the base and a fluted cap.

The *Texas Monument* (fig. 6.4), dedicated in 1961, is similar in style to Henry Hudson Kitson's earlier *Iowa Monument* (fig. 3.3), which it faces across the battle lines, but is unmistakably more modern than the Beaux Arts masterpiece dedicated in 1906. As in Kitson's design, a bronze figure stands before a colonnaded stone wall. The Texas exedra has handsomely proportioned, unfluted, monolithic columns and a frieze of triglyphs and metopes appropriate to the Doric order—classical design components that Kitson would have appreciated. But the angled wings of the exedra and the huge, flat-faced, polished Texas granite panels at the center and

Fig. 6.1. *Peace, Minnesota Monument*

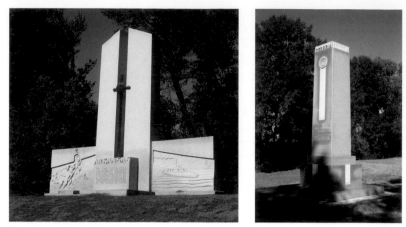

Fig. 6.2. *Arkansas Monument*

Fig. 6.3. *Georgia Monument*

Fig. 6.4. *Texas Monument*

ends of the exedra would have been unthinkable prior to the advent of Modern architecture. The architectural firm of Lundgren and Maurer created a stately memorial in a modern, classically inspired style. It is simple, solemn, understated, well proportioned, and fabricated with durable materials. The yucca plants growing from the lone star–shaped base at the feet of Herring Coe's statue of one of Waul's Texas Legionnaires are an unusual but effective component of the overall design. Their evergreen color, organic form, and spiky texture complement the monument's pinkish-grey granite, especially the rough blocks of the base, with their rounded edges, which are laid with recessed joints, and the eleven broad, low steps (one for each state that seceded) leading to the sculpture. Its inscription reads: "Texas remembers the valor and devotion of her sons. . . ."

Fig. 6.5. *Kentucky Monument*

Two of Kentucky's most famous sons were remembered with statues dedicated at Vicksburg in 2001 (fig. 6.6). Abraham Lincoln and Jefferson Davis were both born in the border state that saw friends and families divided by their loyalties. (The bust of Lincoln's brother-in-law, Confederate Gen. Benjamin Helm, stands nearby.) Since the state strove to commemorate all of its sons who served at Vicksburg, the memorial was placed between the battle lines, near Fort Garrott, on a site selected a century earlier by veterans of the campaign and siege. In keeping with twenty-first-century historic preservation

Fig. 6.6. *Abraham Lincoln* and *Jefferson Davis*, *Kentucky Monument*

ethics, which strive to minimize the memorial's impact on the historic landscape while providing ample space for inscriptions, the bronze figures were set on a sunken, paved plaza enclosed on two adjacent sides by retaining walls that taper from head-high at the apex to knee-high at the ends (fig. 6.5)—rather like the walls of the *Vietnam Memorial* dedicated in 1982 in Washington, D.C. The architecture thus responds to contemporary trends in memorial art and historic preservation, while the statuary stands with the rank and file of the figurative tradition.

7 : The Production of Sculptural Models and Molds

Figurative statuary for monumental sculptures usually begins as drawings or small sketches in clay or wax (figs. 7.1, 7.2) that give form to a sculptor's ideas. For life-sized busts and reliefs, sculptors often start with the full-sized portrait, but life-sized and larger figures are usually first drawn on paper, then modeled in clay design sketches followed by one-quarter- or one-third-scale clay models and eventually a full-sized clay model (fig. 7.3). This process permits the design to be refined as the scale grows. Since clay is heavy and expensive, it is applied in a layer an inch or two thick atop an armature or framework traditionally made from wood lathe and iron or steel pipes. In recent years technological innovation has facilitated construction of armatures using plastic foam and other modern materials, and computer-assisted design programs can now be used to enlarge models.

The months-long sequence from sketch to scale-model to full-sized model enables the artist to construct the armatures for efficient use of the clay. All of the various textures, such as hair, skin, and clothing, as well as the wood grain of a gunstock and the smooth surface of a cannon tube, must be worked into the malleable clay by the sculptor's hands and a few simple tools like rakes and wire loops on small wooden handles.

Once the model is completed, it is cast into a more durable and permanent material. Plaster of Paris traditionally has been used for this purpose because it is inexpensive and easy to work with. For a small model, plaster powder is mixed with water and used to make a mold an inch or so thick around the clay model. Larger molds require wood or metal reinforcement. The mold is made in pieces so that it can be separated, the clay model removed, and then reassembled.

The inside of the mold is sealed and greased, and wet plaster is poured into it to make a positive model. Sometimes wood or metal armatures are inserted into the empty mold to reinforce the plaster models. Once that plaster has set, the mold is removed. The mold is often destroyed in the process, hence its common name—waste mold. The plaster mold and subsequent single plaster cast reproduce the shapes, lines, and textures of the original clay model with great fidelity. The porous plaster model is often shellacked to protect its friable surface.

Fig. 7.1. Design drawing for *Alabama Monument* by Steffen Thomas (Courtesy Steffen Thomas Art Representatives, LP, 4200 Bethany Road, Buckhead, GA 30625)

Fig. 7.2. Small three-dimensional sketch for *Alabama Monument* (Courtesy Steffen Thomas Art Representatives, LP, 4200 Bethany Road, Buckhead, GA 30625)

Plaster scale models are used to "point up" the full-sized clay model. A pointing machine—a three-dimensional pantograph—is used to enlarge the sculptor's forms. The pointing machine is used to correlate hundreds or thousands of points from the plaster scale model to the full-sized clay model, thus translating the forms and proportions of the scale model to the full-sized clay model. In fact, the pointing machine merely shows the

Fig. 7.3. Sculptor Steffen Thomas uses calipers to measure detail on full-scale clay model for the *Alabama Monument* (Courtesy Steffen Thomas Art Representatives, LP, 4200 Bethany Road, Buckhead, GA 30625)

sculptor where, for example, the point on the tip of a soldier's nose should be in space when the scale model is enlarged. The artist must construct the armature and apply the clay in the proper place. Pointing machines can be fitted with rakes, wire loops, or other modeling tools so that the full-sized clay model can be "scraped down" to mimic the shape of the scale model; in effect, the soft clay is carved down in size after being built up on the armature. Making monumental sculpture involves a lengthy process of building up and raking down forms. Although the pointing machine expedites enlargements, the sculptor still needs to refine the forms, add textures, and make adjustments for optical effects that change as the scale grows.

Fig. 7.4. Alabama's Vicksburg Memorial Committee in New York City studio with quarter-scale and full-scale models, both probably in plaster. The sculptor is shown modeling a relief in background. (Courtesy Steffen Thomas Art Representatives, I P, 4200 Bethany Road, Buckhead, GA 30625)

Once the full-sized clay model is completed to the satisfaction of the sculptor and the client (fig. 7.4), a plaster mold and plaster model are produced. For monumental sculptures, these are often made in sections, for practical reasons. The full-sized plaster models are then used by the foundry to make the final bronze castings, which correspond to the plaster model sections. The full-sized plaster models can also be used to reproduce the sculpture in stone. In fact, since the shellacked plaster models are relatively durable, they can be used to make multiple reproductions in stone or bronze.

8 : Bronze Casting with the *Cire Perdue* or Lost Wax Process

Two different techniques are used to make bronze casts—the *cire perdue* (French for lost wax) process and sand molds. These terms refer to the methods and materials used to make models and molds for the molten bronze.

The *cire perdue* process involves the creation of wax models. Small figures and sketch models a few inches in height can be modeled directly in wax, but larger sculptures generally are modeled in clay, which is reproduced in wax using a flexible and reusable rubber mold supported by a plaster "mother mold." The wax casting can then be touched up by the artist, who often uses warm metal tools to work on the cold wax model.

Once the wax model is complete, it is encased in a one-piece investment or mold. Plaster of Paris and grog (pottery shards, pieces of brick, and old fireproof mold material) have been used to make investment molds since the Renaissance, but during the last quarter of the twentieth century ceramic shell molds were introduced. These are thin, lightweight molds that are built up on a wax model in many layers. Very fine ceramic clay forms the first layers, then more coarse ceramic material is applied to strengthen the mold. Ceramic shells are now the most common mold-making technology employed by large fine-arts foundries, but ceramic shell molds can only be used for small sculptures or sections of sculptures that fit in the vats holding the ceramic slurry for the first mold layer. The life-sized figures of Abraham Lincoln and Jefferson Davis on the *Kentucky Monument* (fig. 6.6), dedicated in 2001, were each cast in a half-dozen pieces in ceramic shell molds and then welded together.

To create the three-foot-tall and four-foot-long bronze cast of the quarter-scale model (fig. 8.1) for the *Alabama Monument* in 1951, Modern Art Foundry in New York City made a rubber mold around the plaster model and then made a plaster mother mold in removable sections around the rubber mold. Next, they removed the mother and rubber molds, removed the model, and reassembled the molds. Then they melted wax and poured it into the mold, carefully building up the wax layer to a quarter-inch thick over the interior of the mold. Once the wax dried, they removed the mother molds, peeled off the rubber mold, and attached thin wax rods to the wax model to serve as sprues or conduits to carry the molten bronze into the mold and risers to vent the hot gases.

Fig. 8.1. Quarter-scale model for *Alabama Monument* (Alabama Department of Archives and History, Montgomery, Alabama)

Fig. 8.2. Glowing crucible of molten bronze poised to pour into mold in Modern Art Foundry (Courtesy Steffen Thomas Art Representatives, LP, 4200 Bethany Road, Buckhead, GA 30625)

They pressed numerous iron chaplets (usually long, thin nails) through the wax and left half the chaplet exposed inside the wax to hold the inner mold off the outer mold once the wax was lost. Then they invested the outside of the wax model and filled the core of the mold with wet plaster and grog. The invested wax was baked in a kiln at about 2,000 degrees Fahrenheit for hours to melt the wax and to dry the mold thoroughly while the bronze was melted in a separate furnace. About 100 pounds of molten bronze (fig. 8.2) was poured into the hot, empty mold, filling even the sprues and risers. Within an hour the bronze could be broken

Fig. 8.3. Bronze cast of right side of seated soldier being broken out of investment mold. Notice iron nails or chaplets protruding from the casting. (Courtesy Steffen Thomas Art Representatives, LP, 4200 Bethany Road, Buckhead, GA 30625)

out of the mold (fig. 8.3 shows a section of the full-scale bronze emerging from the mold). The sprues and risers were cut off, the stubs were ground down, the chaplets were drilled out and plugged, and all those spots were "chased" or "cold-worked" with grinders and chisels to match the textures of adjacent surfaces.

Finally, the foundry applied a patina, or color, by brushing chemicals (often liver of sulfur, ferric nitrate, or copper nitrate) on the exterior of the bronze. Usually the bronze is heated with a torch to expedite the chemical reactions that, through repeated applications, slowly change the color of the bronze from the bright "new penny" appearance of raw bronze to various shades of brown or green. A wax coating was applied to protect the bronze surface from atmospheric effects that over time would dull the metal's gloss, change its color, and camouflage its forms through streaks and stains that might mute the commemorative message of the sculpture.

Over the past few decades, innovations in ceramic shell mold-making technology have increased the economy and subsequent popularity of *cire perdue* casting. The lost wax process was favored by sculptors in Europe and America during the nineteenth and twentieth centuries because it permitted them to make adjustments in the wax model quickly and easily. Moreover, it insured that nuances of sculptural forms and textures were replicated accurately in the final bronze casts. And the flexible rubber molds pulled from wax, clay, or plaster models could be used to make dozens of wax models, each of which could be "lost" (the wax is actually reclaimed for reuse) to produce a bronze cast. Still, limitations on the size of wax models caused many sculptors to utilize sand molds to cast their larger statuary, especially in the days before ceramic shell molds and electric arc welding facilitated the molding and assembly of multiple small sections into monumental sculptures.

9 Bronze Casting with the Sand Mold Method

Sand molds enable founders to make monumental sculptures in fewer pieces than is necessary with the lost wax process. Using fewer pieces means less labor-intensive joining and chasing and contributes to the durability of the assembled sculpture because there are fewer pieces that might separate and fewer joins that may show up over time. Joins are hardened by welding and chasing and thus often corrode at a different rate than the rest of the bronze. After many years in the open air, a poorly made or poorly maintained bronze can look like a patchwork quilt rather than the unified sculptural form the artist intended, especially if the joins were not hidden in folds and seams of drapery or other places where natural breaks in sculptural forms disguise them.

Sand molds are made with a fine-grained sand known as French sand or green sand. To make sand molds, sand is packed loosely into a metal flask or frame known as the "drag," and the plaster model is positioned in the sand. Another flask, known as the "cope," is attached to the top of the drag, and sand is rammed firmly around the model. The cope and drag are inverted, the loose sand in the drag is removed, and more sand is rammed into the drag. Wooden dowels are inserted into the loose sand from the surface of the plaster model to the edge of the mold. These will later be burned out in the kiln, leaving sprues for the molten bronze and risers for the hot gases forced from the mold. The cope and the drag are then separated, and the model is removed, leaving a cavity—the hard-packed sand walls of which perfectly mirror the forms, lines, and textures of the plaster model's exterior surface.

If bronze sculptures were solid, that cavity could simply be filled with bronze, but that would be needlessly expensive, and heavy, and the mass of bronze would crack as it cools and shrinks. Consequently, a metal armature is fitted into the cavity and secured to the outer mold in a couple of places. Sand is then packed around the armature, filling the cavity. Next, that core is removed and carefully scraped down or compressed to leave a quarter-inch to three-eighths-inch space between the core and the outer mold in the cope and drag. That thin space will soon be filled with bronze.

Fig. 9.1. Bronze section of full-size casting in the foundry shows a bolt in a flange that will hold two sections together. Workman in rear chases another bronze casting with hammer and punch. (Courtesy Steffen Thomas Art Representatives, LP, 4200 Bethany Road, Buckhead, GA 30625)

Fig. 9.2. Three of four bronze sections of the rear of the *Alabama Monument* are assembled outside the foundry. (Courtesy Steffen Thomas Art Representatives, LP, 4200 Bethany Road, Buckhead, GA 30625)

Fig. 9.3. Gaps around the waist of the female figure of the *Alabama Monument* show where two sections were welded. The top of the bronze group was fitted on the bottom at the foundry but trucked separately to Vicksburg and welded together on site because the sculpture was too large to move in one piece.

As with the lost wax process, the sand mold in the cope and drag, complete with its sand core, is heated in a kiln to make it rock hard, to dry it, and to burn out the wooden dowels. Meanwhile, the bronze is melted in a furnace. It takes hours to melt the bronze and to cure the sand molds, but the bronze pour takes only seconds. The bronze solidifies in a matter of minutes, and the mold can be broken open to see if the core stayed in position and if the bronze flowed into each nook and cranny of the mold.

The sand is collected and reconditioned for reuse. The risers and sprues are cut off, the stubs are ground down and chased, and the bronze is welded to other castings as necessary (figs. 9.1, 9.2, 9.3). Those joins are chased and the bronze assemblage is patinated, waxed, or coated with an acrylic to protect the surface from the weather.

10 Production of Memorial Art in Stone

The granite infantrymen on Ohio regimental monuments (fig. 10.1) began life in clay and plaster just like their bronze comrades in arms. Designers first gave shape to their commemorative ideas by drawing and then sketching the figurative compositions in clay. The small models were enlarged and cast in plaster just as if they were destined for the foundry. They were sent instead to a stone carver who used pointing machines and pneumatic tools to translate the sculptural forms into granite.

Granite is harder than marble and less susceptible to erosion and discoloration. Consequently, since the establishment of national military parks on Civil War battlefields, government regulations have specified that it or limestone be used for monuments, memorials, pedestals, and bases—the marble *Illinois Memorial* at Vicksburg being a conspicuous exception.

Granite's strength, hardness, and durability are functions of its substance and density, characteristics that also result in its great weight and its resistance to cutting and shaping. After the decline of Egyptian civilization in the second millennium BCE, granite was not used for many monuments or other structures built by Western civilizations until the early nineteenth century. By then, innovations in industrial technology facilitated the harvest, transport, cutting, and shaping of stone. Some of the first railroads in the United States were built in and around quarries in New England. By mid-century, steam-powered locomotives moved huge blocks of stone from quarries to nearby cutting sheds. Steam engines

Fig. 10.1. Detail of *47th Ohio Monument*

powered the derricks that lifted the stone as well as the saws, planers, and polishers that cut and honed it. By the early twentieth century, pneumatic hand tools powered by gas and electricity helped stone cutters and carvers create complex shapes and forms in the obdurate stone. Unfortunately, the technology of stone cutting and the popularity of granite buildings and monuments advanced faster than medical knowledge about the health hazards of granite dust and concerns for worker safety. Many quarrymen, stone cutters, and carvers suffered and died from silicosis, the "stone cutter's disease" caused by inhaling silica, the primary component of granite.

Most relatively small granite monuments like the Ohio regimental and battery monuments at Vicksburg (figs. 10.2, 10.3, 10.4) were designed and executed by stone or monument companies, many of which were located near the granite quarries at Westerly, Rhode Island, and Barre, Vermont. These were virtually the only sources in the United States for large blocks of fine-grained granite suitable for carving into figurative sculpture. The Ohio unit memorials at Vicksburg, however, were manufactured by the Hughes Granite and Marble Company, a firm in Clyde, Ohio. Hughes was located between Cleveland and Toledo, with service from four major rail lines. The company operated a very successful business, using stone from quarries in New England (one of which it owned) and the upper Midwest to fabricate monuments, memorials, and mausoleums.

Like most monument companies, Hughes employed carvers, who shaped the sculptural forms, and stone cutters, who made the architectural ornament, as well as mechanics, who maintained the tools and equipment, and carpenters, who crated the completed works. Like a few of the larger firms, Hughes kept an artist on the payroll to design monuments and to create sculptural models, but many monument firms simply purchased designs or models and the rights to reproduce them from independent artists. This is one reason for the similarity of many so-called "stock" Civil War monuments (like the *Monument to the Confederate Dead* in Cedar Hill Cemetery, figs. 2.1, DT82) dedicated around the country in the late nineteenth and early twentieth centuries. Monument companies made multiple carvings from a few models in their possession to satisfy clients' demand for statuary commemorating common soldiers of the North and South. In fact, contrary to popular belief, even at the height of memorialization of the Civil War, around its fortieth anniversary, few monument companies made monuments on speculation and kept them in stock for immediate delivery, but many firms could produce a memorial in a few weeks.

The popularity of statues depicting the common soldier—the acknowledged hero of the Civil War—standing at Parade Rest encouraged their manufacture in large number. Moreover, the fabrication technology enabled talented carvers to deviate from exact copies of their models.

Fig. 10.2. Detail of *114th Ohio Monument*

Moustaches and beards could be added or altered, jackets and coats could be carved instead of shirts, and insignia on belts and hats could be customized to commemorate specific corps, brigades, regiments, or batteries.

Some of the most interesting granite memorials at Vicksburg and other Civil War battlefields are battery monuments shaped like cannon. In some instances (fig. 10.3), cannon on battlefield battery monuments are draped like contemporaneous cemetery memorials featuring shrouded cinerary urns, classical columns, or obelisks—traditional funerary monument forms. Other stone battlefield monuments resemble trophies (fig. 10.4) like those built by the ancient Greeks, who collected weapons and equipment left on the battlefields into sacred piles that stood as memorials to the fallen. By the early twentieth century, technological innovation enabled Americans to memorialize their fallen with durable granite trophies of bedrolls, packs, canteens, cartridge boxes, drums, and trumpets that stand in silent, timeless tribute.

By the early years of the twenty-first century, when Congress expanded the parameters of the campaign and siege of Vicksburg to include the Union attempt to take the city in the summer of 1862, monument design and fabrication technology had evolved into the digital age. When a committee formed in Connecticut to commemorate the unsuccessful 1862 efforts of the Ninth Connecticut regiment to dig a navigational canal through a narrow spit of land opposite Vicksburg and out of reach of the citadel's batteries, they employed computer-assisted design techniques. Graphic designer Kerry Shelden scanned images of the Ninth's flag and

Fig. 10.3. *Eleventh Ohio Battery Monument*

Fig. 10.4. *37th Ohio Monument*

Fig. 10.5. *Connecticut Monument*

historic photos of some of its officers. She digitally altered the faded or damaged images to enhance their legibility and to account for the difference in the ages of some soldiers between 1862 and the dates of their photos. She patched appropriate insignia of rank onto some uniforms to insure the subjects were portrayed as they were in 1862, and she resized or cropped the images into effective designs on the front and back of a tall black granite stele with a polished surface. Next, Stacy Mathieu of Mathieu Memorials and Granite Works of Southington, Connecticut, traced the images on the stone and used a diamond-tipped, electric-powered hand tool to etch the surface, effectively removing the polish and leaving her lines lighter in color and less glossy in texture than the surrounding black stone. The stele was flanked by two shorter slabs of Royal Emerald Green granite—the color emblematic of the Irish heritage of most of the regiment's members—and the vertical elements of the memorial were set atop a concrete plaza whose center is shaped like a map of Connecticut and stained to contrast with the surrounding paving (fig. 10.5). The patrons hoped the map would be visible on images of the memorial and nearby canal site when viewed on Google maps. That degree of detail is not currently available on Google, but the site of the monument is visible beside the abandoned canal.

Numerous images of the memorial's design and fabrication, and a well-edited video of its dedication are on the websites of the designer (www.casualclicks.com) and the Ninth Regiment of Connecticut Volunteers (www.jimlarkin.com/9thRegiment/9thRegimentHome.htm). Such digital documentation of memorial art and architecture at Vicksburg is unusual because virtually all of the other monuments were created before computers revolutionized photography and film-making. Nevertheless, the program for the dedication ceremony closely parallels those of a century earlier—when veterans of the battle participated—and the Internet facilitates documentation of the ceremony in a much more vivid form than the bound publications produced by the state monument commissions in the early twentieth century.

11 Creators of Memorial Art and Architecture at Vicksburg

Although the names of most of the carvers and stone cutters employed by Hughes Granite and Marble Company, as well as those of most of the artisans in other monument companies, foundries, and sculptors' studios, are lost to history, most of the individuals who designed memorial art and architecture for Vicksburg and supervised its creation are known. While these sculptors, architects, and designers did not hit every lick with the mallet or make every mold or every part of each model, they originated the designs, gave form to their ideas, and coordinated production of the finished products. Like architects (who do not hammer, plumb, or pour concrete), the designers of monuments, memorials, and commemorative statuary are justly credited for their creations.

Several architects and sculptors whose work graces the battlefield at Vicksburg were well known and respected by their peers and the public during their lifetimes. Albert Randolph Ross (*Pennsylvania Monument,* fig. 11.1) and Liance Cottrell (*Wisconsin Monument,* DT12) were successful architects. Cottrell, who specialized in monument and residential design, also created the stately *Pennsylvania Monument* at Gettysburg (1910), a domed structure on the scale of the *Illinois Memorial* at Vicksburg. Herbert Adams (*Michigan Monument,* DT7, DT8) and Adolph Alexander Weinman (*Lt. Col. William Vilas,* fig. 11.2) were elected by their colleagues as presidents of the National Sculpture Society, a professional association similar to the American Institute of Architects. Edward Potter (*Gen. John McClernand,* fig. 15.3), whose specialty was horses, was trusted by the dean of early-twentieth-century monumental sculpture—Daniel Chester French—to model the mounts for his equestrian portraits. Potter also created numerous portraits, including the handsome equestrian *Gen. Henry Slocum* at Gettysburg (1902), on his own. William Sievers created the equestrian portrait of *Gen. Lloyd Tilghman* (fig. 3.1) and a portrait of Gen. Robert E. Lee seated on Traveler for the *Virginia Monument* at Gettysburg (1917).

Sievers operated his studio in Richmond, Virginia, but during the early twentieth century most sculptors worked in New York, New England, or Philadelphia to be part of the larger art world and to have easy access to fine-arts foundries, most of which were located in New York, Philadelphia,

Fig. 11.1. *Pennsylvania Monument*

and Providence, Rhode Island. Chicago was also a popular place for artists, especially after the World's Columbian Exposition in 1893. Some of the sculptors who helped create the temporary, neoclassical "White City" in Chicago, under the direction of master sculptor Lorado Taft, later made statuary for monuments to Midwestern subjects erected at Vicksburg.

In addition to supervising the mammoth sculptural program for the "White City," Taft ran an active studio in which Frederick Hibbard (*Grant*), Leonard Crunelle (*Logan,* fig. 11.3), Victor Holm (*Missouri Monu-*

Fig. 11.2. *Lt. Col. William Vilas Monument*

ment), and other talented sculptors trained. In that studio Taft made the statue of Admiral Porter (fig. 11.4) for the *U.S. Navy Memorial.* Taft also wrote the first comprehensive history of American sculpture; it was published in 1903 with an enlarged edition in 1924. He chronicled the careers of America's greatest sculptors and touched on the life and work of hundreds more, praising many of the men who made commemorative art at Vicksburg. He mentioned William Couper (*Peace* on *Minnesota Monument,* fig. 6.1; *Adm. Andrew Foote,* DT36, DT37, on the *U.S. Navy Memorial;* and the bust of Gen. Isham Garrott, figs. 14.2, 14.3); Francis

Edwin Elwell (*Rhode Island Monument*, DT20); Frederick Ernst Triebel (*Mississippi Monument*, DT57, DT58); and George Brewster (two statues, eight busts, and thirteen reliefs); as well as Solon Borglum (brother of Gutzon Borglum of Mount Rushmore and Stone Mountain fame); and Roland Hinton Perry (six busts and two reliefs at Vicksburg plus the Union and Confederate soldiers who shake hands atop the *New York State Peace Monument* dedicated on Lookout Mountain in Chattanooga in 1910).

Taft also admired the art of Henry Hudson Kitson (fig. 12.2) and his wife, Theo Alice Ruggles Kitson (fig. 12.3). H. H. Kitson won commissions for the elaborately ornamented *Iowa Monument* and statues of *Gen. Stephen Dill Lee* (fig. 16.1), *Jefferson Davis* (DT60, DT61), and *Adm. David Farragut* (DT35) on the *U.S. Navy Memorial*. He also modeled four busts and two relief portraits for Vicksburg, but Theo A. R. Kitson created an astounding 52 reliefs and 19 busts for Vicksburg—many more than any other artist. In addition, Theo assisted Henry with the extensive sculptural program for the *Iowa Monument,* and she made the *Massachusetts Monument* (fig. 11.5), an energetic bronze figure depicting a youthful *Volunteer of 1861* who strides confidently off to war.

Taft's commentary on Theo A. R. Kitson is worth reproducing at length because it illuminates the achievement of this remarkable woman artist who competed successfully in the almost exclusively male world of monumental sculpture in the United States in the early twentieth century:

> She received an honorable mention at the Paris Exposition of 1889, and a similar distinction at the Salon the following year. Mrs. Kitson is one of the three women members of the National Sculpture Society. Her talent is robust, and she attacks fearlessly the problems of monumental statuary. Her *Volunteer* erected in 1902 as a soldiers' monument at Newburyport, Massachusetts, has been justly applauded, and will be reproduced as the Massachusetts monument upon the battlefield at Vicksburg. In the presence of this spirited and ably composed work one is almost compelled to qualify the somewhat sweeping assertion that no woman has as yet modeled the male figure to look like a man. If not a powerful man, the *Volunteer* is at least a most satisfactory representation of adolescent youth.

Kitson's *Volunteer* was so popular that it was cast a total of ten times for different Civil War memorials in New York, New England, and California. It is unusual for monumental statuary to be reproduced more than once or twice, but the *Volunteer* is not unique in that respect. Kitson also crafted a heroic-scale figure of a *Hiker* (the term designating soldiers of the Spanish-American War who trudged through steamy jungles in Cuba and the Philippines), which was replicated 51 times. In short, Theo

Fig. 11.3. *Gen. John Logan Monument*

Fig. 11.4. *Adm. David Porter, U.S. Navy Memorial*

Fig. 11.5. *The Volunteer, Massachusetts Monument*

Fig. 11.6. *First and Third Mississippi, African Descent Monument*

Alice Ruggles Kitson produced more sculpture for Vicksburg than any other artist, and her Vicksburg work formed a larger proportion of the artist's total oeuvre than did the Vicksburg work of other artists. Still, it represents but a small part of her lifetime work.

Subsequent to the great age of American monuments and memorials that ended shortly after publication of Taft's expanded edition of *The History of American Sculpture* in 1924, few artists have made art for Vicksburg because few subjects associated with the campaign and siege remained to be commemorated. Steffen Thomas, a European-born and -trained artist who spent most of his career in Georgia, modeled the *Alabama Monument* and a portrait of Alabama Gen. John Forney, both dedicated in 1951. Gary Casteel, a contemporary artist who specializes in Civil War subjects, modeled the figures of Kentuckians Abraham Lincoln and Jefferson Davis for the *Kentucky Monument* (fig. 6.6), dedicated in 2001. Casteel also made an equestrian portrait of Gen. James Longstreet for Gettysburg (1998), as well as a few other heroic-scale figures and many small-scale bronzes, some of which are reproductions of older Civil War battlefield statuary cast to raise money for preservation of Civil War battlefields and memorials. J. Kim Sessums, a Mississippi artist who won the commission to commemorate the First and Third Mississippi regiments of soldiers of African descent (fig. 11.6), also produced small bronze portraits of several famous Americans, plus a few life-sized busts and figures—all while maintaining a career as a physician.

Over the years, scores of sculptors, architects, and designers have created memorial art and architecture to mark the historic site of the campaign and siege of Vicksburg. Whether academically trained, apprenticed, or self-taught, all wrestled with their subjects—men engaged in a classic military struggle—and attempted to memorialize those men, their courage, and their devotion to duty with figurative sculpture and architectural elements that evoke respect for their sacrifice and achievements.

12 Sculptors of Memorial Art at Vicksburg

Most sculptors signed their work on its base, often on the back or another inconspicuous spot, such as the lower corner of a relief (fig. 12.1). An artist's signature and sometimes the date can often be found if one looks carefully on the vertical face of the back or side of an integral bronze plinth of a bust or statue. Signatures are usually rather small. Signatures may be inscribed in the clay original, or an artist's name may be stamped or engraved into the cold bronze. Signatures are more easily seen on bronzes that have been cleaned and waxed because their glossy surfaces show the contrasts between broad surfaces and incisions more clearly than do the more matte surfaces of unwaxed, often discolored, bronzes. Stone statuary rarely has artist names carved into its surfaces.

Sculptors who made art for VNMP

> Adams, Herbert (1858–1945), *Michigan Monument*
> Borglum, Solon H. (1868–1922), 5 busts, 1 relief
> Brewster, George T. (1862–1943), 2 statues, 8 busts, 18 reliefs
> Casteel, Gary (born 1946), 2 statues on *Kentucky Monument*
> Cianfarani, Aristide Berto (1895–1960), 1 bust
> Coe, Herring (1907–1999), figure on *Texas Monument*
> Couper, William (1853–1942), *Minnesota Monument*, 2 statues, 3 busts
> Crunelle, Leonard (1872–1944), *General Logan*
> Elwell, Francis Edwin (1858–1922), *Rhode Island Monument*, 2 statues, 1 bust, 2 reliefs
> Ganiere, George E. (1865–1935), 2 busts, 6 reliefs
> Hibbard, Frederick C. (1881–1950), *General Grant* equestrian statue, eagle on *Illinois Memorial*, 1 bust
> Holm, Victor S. (1876–1935), *Missouri Monument*, 6 reliefs
> Kitson, Henry Hudson (1863–1947, fig. 12.2), *Iowa Monument*, 3 statues, 4 busts, 2 reliefs
> Kitson, Theo Alice Ruggles (1876–1932, fig. 12.3), *Massachusetts Monument*, assisted with *Iowa Monument*, 19 busts, 52 reliefs

Fig. 12.1. Detail of relief panel on *Iowa Monument* showing sculptor's name and foundry mark

Loester, Julius C. (unknown), executed *Wisconsin Monument*
    statuary to Cottrell's design
Lopez, Charles A. (1869–1906), 5 reliefs on *Pennsylvania Monument*
McKenzie, R. Tait (1867–1938), 2 busts flanking walk to *Pennsylvania Monument*
Milione, Louis (1884–1955), 1 bust, 1 relief
Mulligan, Charles J. (1866–1916), 3 busts on *Illinois Memorial*
Newman, Allen G. (1875–1940), 2 reliefs
Perry, Roland Hinton (1870–1941), 6 busts, 2 reliefs
Potter, Edward Clark (1857–1923), *General McClernand* equestrian statue
Quinn, Edmond T. (1868–1929), 1 statue, 1 bust
Rieker, Albert George (unknown), 1 bust
Saville, Bruce W. (1893–1938), 3 reliefs

Fig. 12.2. Henry Hudson Kitson with ball of clay and rake, ca. 1900 (Henry Hudson and Theo Alice Ruggles Kitson papers, Archives of American Art, Smithsonian Institution)

Fig. 12.3. Theo Alice Ruggles modeling bust in clay, ca. 1890 (Henry Hudson and Theo Alice Ruggles Kitson papers, Archives of American Art, Smithsonian Institution)

Schaaf, Anton (1869–1943), 1 statue, 7 busts, 4 reliefs

Sessums, J. Kim (born 1958), *First and Third Mississippi Regiments, African Descent*

Sievers, Frederick William (1872–1966), *General Tilghman* equestrian statue

Taft, Lorado (1860–1936), 1 statue on *U.S. Navy Monument*

Thomas, Steffen (1906–90), *Alabama Monument*, 1 statue

Triebel, Frederick (1865–1944), *Mississippi Monument*

Weinman, Adolph Alexander, (1870–1952), *Colonel Vilas*, 1 relief

Additional information on these sculptors may be found in Appendix B.

13 : Bronze Foundries
of Memorial Art at Vicksburg

Like artist signatures, foundry marks are often found on the base or back (fig. 13.1) of bronzes. They may be stamped in the bronze or inscribed in the clay or wax original. On large monuments, multiple foundries may be employed in order to meet a tight production timetable. Some bronze relief panels on the *Iowa Monument* were cast by Roman Bronze Works (fig. 13.2), others by Bureau Brothers (fig. 13.3), and still others by Gorham (fig. 13.4)—a company better known for its silver. Several bronzes at Vicksburg were cast by Tiffany Studios—a firm famed for its glass and decorative arts but that also cast bronze for a short time. There may be more monumental bronzes by Tiffany at Vicksburg than in any other public collection; most of Tiffany's large bronze works were for ecclesiastical settings.

During the first quarter of the twentieth century, American fine arts foundries produced handsome, durable castings whose quality compares favorably with the best European work of the nineteenth century. From about 1850 to 1900, first German and then French foundries established a standard of excellence in fabricating monumental bronzes that has been widely recognized. The fine-quality castings of many early American foundries such as John Williams, Bureau Brothers, Gorham, Roman Bronze, and Tiffany are less well-known. American foundries have continued to excel technically and artistically, especially during the public art boom of the past forty years.

Foundries known to have made bronzes in VNMP

> Alloyed Metal & Mfg. Co., location unknown
> American Art Bronze, Chicago, IL
> ART [Art Research Technology] Foundry, Lancaster, PA
> Bureau Brothers, Philadelphia, PA
> Chicago Art Bronze Works, Chicago, IL
> Florentine Brotherhood Foundry, Chicago, IL
> Gorham Company Founders, Providence, RI
> G. Vignali Foundry, Florence, Italy
> John Williams, New York, NY

Fig. 13.1. Gorham Co. foundry mark on back of base of *General Sanborn* bust

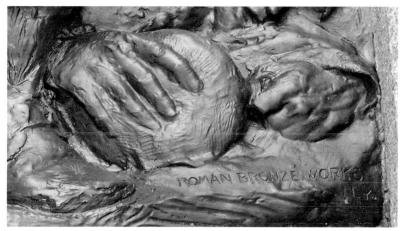

Fig. 13.2. Roman Bronze Works foundry mark on relief on *Iowa Monument*

Fig. 13.3. Bureau Brothers foundry mark on relief on *Iowa Monument*

Fig. 13.4. Henry H. Kitson signature and Gorham Co. foundry mark on relief on *Iowa Monument*

Jules Berchem, Chicago, IL
Laser and Co., unknown location
Modern Art Foundry, New York, NY
Roman Bronze Works, New York, NY
Tiffany Studios, New York, NY
Weston Studio Foundry, Santa Fe, NM

Additional information about these foundries may be found in Appendix B.

14 : Preservation of Monuments and Memorials at Vicksburg

Since the 1970s, custodians of outdoor sculpture have realized that exposure to the environment has deteriorated bronze, marble, and other materials used in monuments, memorials, and other forms of public art. Only granite, the rock of ages, seems impervious to modern atmospheric pollutants, like oxides of nitrogen and sulfur, which result from burning coal, oil, and gasoline. Those compounds are concentrated near busy roadways and industrial areas, and they are carried aloft from power plants.

In fact, one of the most corrosive forms of acidic deposition occurs when dry particulate pollution mixes with moisture on sculptures wet with morning dew or saturated with the high humidity typical of the South. Chemical reactions are accelerated by heat from the sun, which can make bronzes too hot to touch in the summer. Under these conditions bronzes corrode, discolor, and streak. The products of bronze corrosion are more water-soluble in acidic environments, so they are subsequently washed off by rain, exposing the underlying metal to corrosion and carrying the corrosion products onto stone bases that become discolored if they are made of porous materials like limestone or marble. Marble also suffers from atmospheric exposure, slowly eroding under the best of conditions and rapidly eroding under acidic conditions, which dissolve the stone's softer components, thus permitting its harder granules to be washed or brushed off.

In the 1970s, custodians, curators, conservators, and conservation scientists began to explore ways to protect outdoor sculpture from the environment, to preserve its visual and material character, and in some cases to restore its original appearance. Techniques have evolved to clean bronze with high-pressure water blasting and various airborne abrasives like ground walnut shells (also used to clean jet engines), baking soda, and tiny glass beads. Over time, techniques like pressure washing and walnut-shell blasting have proven most popular because they remove loose corrosion but not the well-adhered base layer of bronze patina. They thus preserve more vintage material than more aggressive media like glass beads, which actually peen the metal, arguably making it more resistant to subsequent corrosion but necessitating complete repatination. Patination

Fig. 14.1. Tom Podnar hot-waxing *The Volunteer* in 2009 (Courtesy McKay Lodge Fine Arts Conservation)

Fig. 14.2. *General Garrott* bust before conservation

Fig. 14.3. *General Garrott* bust after cleaning and waxing

Fig. 14.4. *Lt. Col. William Vilas* after cleaning and waxing

is a chemical process that occurs at some expense to the metal because it converts metal from one form and color to another (like a copper penny that goes brown then green over time) rather than merely painting or coating it. In recent years, conservators have learned how to repatinate portions of an aged outdoor bronze cleaned with water or walnut shells in order to unify the patina without stripping the entire sculpture.

Natural and synthetic waxes or acrylic coatings like Incralac (a product developed to inhibit copper corrosion) are usually applied to cleaned bronzes to protect them from water and atmospheric pollution. Corrosion inhibitors like BTA (benzotriazole) may be added to waxes, and waxes are often applied to heated bronzes (fig. 14.1) for greater penetration of the porous metal. Waxing also restores the glossy, jewel-like quality that most monumental outdoor sculptures displayed when new. Moreover, wax visually unifies sculptural surfaces, reducing the contrast between streaks and discoloration caused by corrosion (compare figs. 14.2, 14.3, 3.2).

When most of the commemorative art was made for Vicksburg, sculptors anticipated that their bronzes would weather and age as monumental sculptures had done in Europe for years; however, they did not expect the deterioration to accelerate as it did in the twentieth century due to the dramatic increase in the use of fossil fuels. They knew that bronze was physically durable, but that its visual character could suffer from corrosion. Since their aesthetic employs subtle textural variations and contrasts of light and shade, differential corrosion of boldly exposed and sheltered surfaces can alter the art's appearance to the extent that the sculpture's memorial message is muted. Streaks and stains can camouflage sculptural forms, rendering the most noble allegorical figure forlorn, the most handsome portrait head masked, or the most expressive symbolic composition illegible. Conservation tools as simple as gentle detergents and wax can restore the visual integrity of sculptors' memorial art and preserve historic monuments for future generations to see and appreciate.

Fortunately, the outdoor bronzes in Vicksburg are in relatively good condition, and VNMP has engaged in a multi-year program to clean and wax its many commemorative bronzes. Several state monuments (Alabama, Iowa, Mississippi, Missouri, Massachusetts, Rhode Island, and Texas), all three equestrian statues, and the *U.S. Navy Memorial* were treated prior to 2010, as were all of the statues (fig. 14.4), busts, and reliefs on the park's South Loop. We can hope that more states, private donors, and the National Park Service will continue to support the preservation of memorial art at Vicksburg.

15 Equestrian Portraits at Vicksburg

Is there any truth to the story that the number of hooves a horse has on the ground indicates how the rider in that equestrian portrait died? Not really. In the early twentieth century, sculptor William Sievers responded to a query from the superintendent of Gettysburg National Military Park with a letter flatly denying that sculptors conformed to any such formula in designing equestrian portraits. He also pointed out that the action of the horse, whether rearing, racing, or standing calmly, contributed to the portrait of the rider. Although the feet of horses in Gettysburg's early equestrian portraits do fit a pattern subsequently noted by Gettysburg historians, that pattern was a coincidence rather than a design consideration.

For example, the equestrian portrait of Confederate Gen. "Stonewall" Jackson at Manassas shows Jackson standing like a stone wall at the first battle of Bull Run. All of the horse's feet are set squarely on the ground. But the equestrian portrait of Jackson in Charlottesville shows the general's mount in motion, with one front and one hind hoof off the ground (although attached almost invisibly for the structural stability of the heavy sculpture). Stonewall and his steed stride forward aggressively like the general's troops, who referred to themselves as "foot cavalry" because of their frequent forced marches around Virginia. The two monuments commemorate different aspects of Jackson, and the actions of the horses are key to those depictions. One memorial captures Stonewall's stubborn resolve to stand fast; the other his cunning initiative to outmarch, outflank, and outfight the enemy.

At Vicksburg, Gen. Lloyd Tilghman's bronze steed (fig. 15.1) rears, while those of Grant (fig. 15.2) and McClernand (fig. 15.3) stand quietly as their riders survey the battlefield from behind the lines. Tilghman was killed instantly at Champion Hill while manning cannon that were about to be captured or destroyed. He was struck by a shell fragment that nearly tore his body apart. The small tear in his uniform just below his heart is less evident than the wild action of his horse at the moment of the explosion or the gesture of the general's widespread arms and upraised sword. Those aspects of the figural composition illustrate the violent impact of the artillery round that killed Tilghman. One must look closely to see that

Fig. 15.1. *Gen. Lloyd Tilghman Monument*

Fig. 15.2. *Gen. Ulysses Grant Monument*

Fig. 15.3. *Gen. John McClernand Monument*

Tilghman's facial expression reveals an immediate reaction to the mortal wound (DT55, DT56). All of those details, large and small, contribute to Sievers's portrayal of a courageous commander at a dramatic moment. Beaux Arts sculptors often chose to depict dramatic moments in the lives of their subjects because the subjects were frequently known for those specific events and because those moments often provided distinctive images to capture for all time in bronze and stone. Although many of the men portrayed at Vicksburg died violent deaths similar to Tilghman's, few of Vicksburg's memorials depict that violence as explicitly as the *Tilghman Monument*.

In sharp contrast to the action of Tilghman and his steed, Grant and his horse stand still and quiet. Like better-known equestrian portraits of Grant by William Merwin Shrady (1922) at the foot of the Capitol in

Washington, D.C., and the Philadelphia statue (1897) by Daniel Chester French and Edward Potter, Hibbard's horse and rider portray a sturdy leader, a compact figure set squarely upon a handsome horse that waits patiently just as Grant and his army did for 47 days at Vicksburg. The silhouette of the sculpture is closed and contained rather than open as with that of Tilghman. Hibbard's composition is sited where Grant's headquarters tent stood during the campaign and siege, but the sculpture and its flanking exedral benches are a little cramped on this hilltop site. The absence of a paved plaza to unify the pedestal and benches accentuates the isolation of the sculpture on its tall pedestal from the flanking seats, and the steep hillsides limit viewers' perspectives to low angles, especially from the front and proper right side of the sculpture (see fig. 4.6). Still, Hibbard's calm figural composition successfully conveys the general's commanding presence and fortitude, even if his attire seems more uniform than one might expect given his reputation to disregard regulations regarding personal appearance.

Potter's *McClernand* has more vitality than Hibbard's *Grant* but less drama than Sievers's *Tilghman*. That vitality is expressed clearly through the horse's alert stance and posture. All four feet are on the ground, but the horse's muscles are taut, poised for action. His head is held high. His ears are up and twisted in opposite directions, monitoring the cacophony of noise that surrounds him and his rider when McClernand's troops assault the Confederate lines on May 22. McClernand sits erect in the saddle with his fist clinched against his hip, arm akimbo. The pose suggests strength, boldness, and hopefulness as he gazes intently across the field to the Railroad Redoubt that his troops briefly captured before being repulsed by reinforcements. Within days of that engagement, Grant relieved McClernand of his command and replaced him with Gen. Edward O. C. Ord, whose pedestrian statue stands nearby, but modern scholars attribute McClernand's demotion less to his performance on May 22 than to long-term friction between career military officers and political appointees like McClernand. None of that backstory is evident in Potter's masterful equestrian, but historians, horse lovers, and art aficionados agree on the prowess of this portrait. The accuracy of McClernand's likeness, the subtle actions of his horse, and an apt depiction of the most dramatic moment in this man's experience during the campaign and siege of Vicksburg speak volumes about the portrait's subject, the artist, and the epic struggle for the Gibraltar of the Confederacy.

So, in short, any relationship between the number of hooves the horse in an equestrian portrait has on the ground and the way the rider died may be merely coincidental, but the sculptor's portrait of a horse definitely contributes to the portrait of the rider.

16 Portrait Figures at Vicksburg

All seventeen of the full-length portrait statues at Vicksburg depict their subjects realistically. A couple do so with verve. Henry H. Kitson's *Gen. Stephen Dill Lee* (fig. 16.1) and Adolph A. Weinman's *Lt. Col. William Vilas* (fig. 16.2) are animated portrayals of these Vicksburg veterans, both of whom lived to enjoy prosperous postwar careers. Vilas (1840–1908) taught law at the University of Wisconsin, served in the state assembly and U.S. Senate, and was appointed Postmaster General and Secretary of the Interior. Lee (1833–1908) became president of what is now Mississippi State University, commander in chief of the United Confederate Veterans, and chairman of the VNMP Commission, the only Confederate veteran elected to chair a national military park commission.

A few days before his death in 1908, Lee posed for a photograph at the sculpture site, the spot from which he had watched Union troops assault his line on May 22, 1863. Perhaps Lee himself struck this noble pose; maybe it was the sculptor's idea for him to hold his drawn sword with both hands—an unusual composition that plays on the sharp contrast between the steel blade and Lee's gauntleted fists. Beaux Arts aesthetics, which Kitson studied and practiced, made the most of such textural contrasts and variations in light and shade caused by folds in fabric, shoe leather, and hat felt. Kitson created a masterful portrait of a man he knew through his extensive interactions with the park commission in Lee's later years, and he placed it on a rough-faced granite pedestal, the coarseness of which provides a foil to the general's trim features.

Fig. 16.1. *Gen. Stephen Dill Lee Monument*

Weinman may not have known Vilas. Certainly he did not know him during the war because the sculptor was born in 1870, in Germany. He immigrated at age ten, studied in

Fig. 16.2. General view of *Lt. Col. William Vilas Monument*

16.3. *Lt. Col. William Vilas* statue and bronze cannon tube on cheek block of plaza

Fig. 16.4. Inscribed pedestal of *Lt. Col. William Vilas Monument*

New York at the Art Students League and Cooper Union, assisted Augustus Saint-Gaudens and Daniel Chester French, and executed designs for U.S. coinage, including the *Mercury* dime and *Walking Liberty* half dollar. He became a favorite sculptor of the renowned Beaux Arts architectural firm McKim, Mead, and White, but for his memorial to Lt. Col. Vilas, funded by the subject's wealthy family, he teamed with Albert Randolph Ross, another respected architect whose *Pennsylvania Monument* stands at Vicksburg. The architectural setting for Vilas is extraordinary—an exquisitely propor-

Fig. 16.5. Artist signature and date on base of Lt. Col. William Vilas Monument

Fig. 16.6. Foundry mark on base of Lt. Col. William Vilas Monument

tioned and expertly tooled pink granite plaza with thirteen broad, short steps made alternately with one or two large, flat stones. Flanking the stairs are cheek blocks ornamented with pairs of laurel wreathes and topped with historic Civil War cannon tubes, the aged brass of which echoes the bronze tones of the statuary (fig. 16.3). The figure is striking. With one hand on his sword, the other hitched in his belt, the colonel stands with his left foot raised slightly atop a rock—not unlike Kitson's *Lee*. The handsome Vilas, coat pulled tightly across his broad chest, wears his hat cocked low over his eyes. His command of the 23rd Wisconsin is chronicled on the face of the granite pedestal in stately, capital, serif letters, each line spread evenly across the stone in a manner introduced by Saint-Gaudens and Stanford White (fig. 16.4), and the dates are recorded in Roman numerals as was popular at the time. In fact, the sculptor dated his work on the bronze plinth below the tree stump in Roman numerals (fig. 16.5). Characteristic of his consistency and attention to detail, his name (fig. 16.5) and that of the foundry (fig. 16.6) are also inscribed in the same classic font.

17 Portrait Busts at Vicksburg

Most of the busts at Vicksburg depict brigade and division commanders (fig. 17.1), many of whom did not survive the campaign and siege. A Union sharpshooter killed Isham Garrott on June 17 while he commanded earthworks built to buttress the lines near the Railroad Redoubt. He died without knowing he had just been promoted to brigadier general. His troops subsequently named the works Fort Garrott in memory of the popular colonel of the 20th Alabama. In 1909 his two sons donated the bust by William Couper, which was, by necessity, modeled from photographs. Garrott was a big man, about six feet six inches tall, with broad shoulders and a full beard. His stature is less evident in Couper's portrait (figs. 14.2, 14.3) than his determination, which shows in his tight lips and the penetrating eyes shaded by the broad brim of his hat. Like many sculptors trained in the Beaux Arts tradition, Couper draped Garrott's open coat over his shoulders to add visual variety to the double-breasted uniform. He included the three stars of a Confederate brigadier general on Garrott's collar due to the national military park rule that subjects be depicted with their highest rank attained during the battle commemorated. The bust stands near the site of Garrott's death.

Fig. 17.1. Busts near *Kentucky Monument*

Fig. 17.2. *VNMP Commissioner William Rigby*

Fig. 17.3. Inscription on the back of the bronze bust of VNMP Commissioner *William Rigby*

Immediately opposite Fort Garrott stands the bust of *William T. Rigby* (fig. 17.2), a lieutenant in the 24th Iowa who survived the war and served as resident commissioner of VNMP from 1899 until his death in 1929, and as chairman from 1901 until 1928. Rigby does not wear the bars of a lieutenant, or even those of a captain, a rank he attained in October 1863. In fact, he does not wear a military uniform. And he is not depicted as a young warrior, but as a balding elder in a business suit with his Grand Army of the Republic pin in his lapel. Rigby's greatest service to his country was through the Vicksburg National Military Park Commission of the U.S. War Department. He was an able administrator and tireless advocate for the park. He traveled, politicked, and wrote countless letters to state legislatures, veterans groups, and families of soldiers and sailors to encourage them to mark the battlefield with monuments and memorials. He was the government's liaison with sculptors and architects, urging them to create inspiring art, to use the best materials possible, and to site them in the appropriate places—all to great success. As the words engraved on the pedestal indicate, Rigby's bust was "given by his friends." As the inscription in clay on the lower back of the portrait (fig. 17.3) proclaims, the sculpture

Fig. 17.4. *Col. Thomas Waul Monument,* one of Theo Alice Ruggles Kitson's 19 busts at VNMP, is one of the most lifelike and dramatic portraits on the field. Most sculptors agree that the best figurative sculptures "have breath," jargon for a living, breathing facsimile of the subject. Kitson's *Waul* certainly "has breath."

is "by his friend, H. H. Kitson," the sculptor of the *Iowa Monument,* a bust of Iowa's war governor Samuel Kirkwood, the statues of Jefferson Davis, Gen. Stephen D. Lee, Adm. David Farragut (on the *U.S. Navy Memorial*), and four other busts. Kitson knew Rigby well, and he created a loving portrait of the man who made many friends during his long career commemorating the heroes of Vicksburg. In the course of that career, Rigby became one of the heroes of Vicksburg, if not for his courage and military prowess during the war, then certainly for the preservation of the battlefield and the commemoration of Vicksburg's soldiers and sailors.

18 : Portrait Reliefs at Vicksburg

Artists have long recognized that relief sculpture is a difficult format that involves the challenges of both painting and sculpture. Moreover, most of Vicksburg's portrait reliefs were modeled from photographs of men who died during the war or in the intervening decades prior to the park's establishment in 1899. It is a challenge for any artist to portray someone they never met, someone who is unable to sit for a portrait so that the artist can glimpse their mannerisms, vitality, and personality. Producing a lifelike relief portrait is even more difficult when time is tight for the artist, as it was for many who contracted to supply bronze portrait reliefs on the basis of their low bid for the work. As memorialization of regimental, battery, and brigade commanders neared completion in the 1910s, the park commission requested sealed bids for groups of busts and reliefs from sculptors whose work they respected. Consequently, some of Vicksburg's portrait reliefs are what the artists called "pot boilers," small jobs that kept the family fed between major commissions. In the early twentieth century, when $1,000 would buy a new automobile, life-sized reliefs by reputable artists might be had for a couple hundred dollars.

Fig. 18.1. *Colonel Manning Force Monument*   Fig. 18.2. *Lt. Col. Sidney Griffin Monument*

Many sculptors working under these conditions still managed to create impressive portrait reliefs. Like Theo Alice Ruggles Kitson, who made many reliefs for Vicksburg in a short time, some artists created a reusable flat plaster panel framed with a raised laurel leaf border (fig. 18.1). On this they modeled the subject's flattened head and shoulders in clay. Inscriptions could be set on the plaster panel with reusable metal letters that were available in a variety of sizes and fonts. Supplemental information such as the name of a donor or an officer's subsequent military history could be added

Fig. 18.3. *Col. Allen Thomas Monument*

on a separate bronze text panel affixed below the portrait. Other artists preferred a recessed background that provided more room for figurative forms to project in higher relief (fig. 18.2).

Regardless of the techniques involved, each artist attempted to replicate the officer's appearance, to convey a sense of his vitality and nobility, and to record his rank and position during the campaign and siege of Vicksburg. Once cast in bronze, the reliefs, which were all the same size, were shipped to Vicksburg, where they were mounted on simple stone stelae that varied slightly in shape over the two decades that the park pursued its program to portray all the officers ranking at or above the battery and brigade level.

19 Illustrated Driving Tour of Selected Group and Portrait Monuments

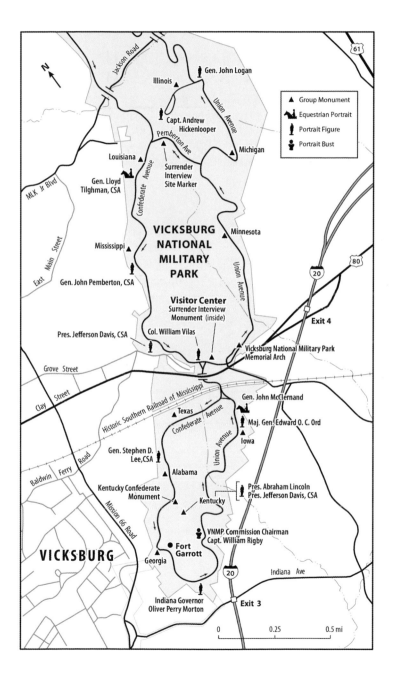

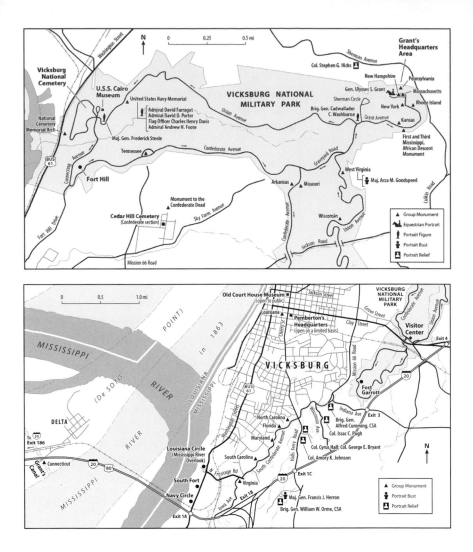

The following pages contain illustrations and information about the major monuments and memorials at VNMP. They appear in the book in the order in which they are seen by viewers driving the VNMP tour route, which starts at the Visitor Center.

In addition to the Driving Tour maps found here, park visitors may want to obtain a free fold-out park map from the park entrance kiosk or Visitor Center.

To locate images and information regarding specific monuments and memorials, please consult the index.

DT1. *Surrender Interview Monument* on original site with cast-iron fence, 1866–67 (courtesy Vicksburg National Military Park)

DT2. *Surrender Interview Monument* in National Cemetery, late nineteenth century (courtesy Vicksburg National Military Park)

DT3. *Surrender Interview Monument,* 1864, inside Visitor Center

This marble obelisk, which was originally intended as a Mexican War memorial, was obtained from a defunct local stone company by Union soldiers in the occupation force. They engraved it incorrectly, citing the interview date as July 4, and set it on the site of the interview between generals Grant and Pemberton to mark the first anniversary of Vicksburg's surrender. It was soon vandalized by souvenir hunters, so in 1867 it was moved to the train station and later to the National Cemetery. The interview site was then marked by the engraved cannon tube currently on the site. In 1940 the obelisk was moved back to its original site and in 1988 to storage briefly before being placed in the Visitor Center in the 1990s. The engraved cannon tube was lost after 1940 but was subsequently found in Charleston, South Carolina, and returned to Vicksburg in the 1980s.

Only three Civil War battlefield monuments definitely predate this one: *Bartow Monument* at Manassas, the *Thirty-Second Indiana Monument* erected at Munfordville, Kentucky, and *Hazen's Brigade Monument* at Stone's River. The *Stovall Monument* at Manassas was cut in November 1861 but not erected until after April 1862, and possibly not until after the war. Union monuments at Groveton and Henry House on the Manassas battlefields were erected in May and June 1865. The *43rd Wisconsin and 180th Ohio Monument,* now in Stone's River National Cemetery, inscribed 1865, was placed by active-duty troops, but its placement date is unknown.

DT4. *Vicksburg National Military Park Memorial Arch,* William Lawhon, architect, 1920

The memorial arch was constructed with money left over from the federally funded veteran reunion known as the National Memorial Celebration and Peace Jubilee at Vicksburg in 1917. When the Stone Mountain granite arch was completed in 1920 it spanned Clay Street, but it became a traffic hazard and was moved into the park in 1967.

DT5. *Peace, Minnesota Monument,*
  William Couper, 1907
DT6. *Minnesota Monument,* William
  Couper, 1907

Couper's classically draped and idealized woman, the sculptural exemplar of Peace, holds a laurel wreath and steadies a large sword by her side. The sword is neither sheathed nor drawn for battle, but rests with its point in the ground. This design was worked out between the sculptor and the committee, which clearly expressed its view that the monument "should in some striking manner suggest the idea of peace."

DT7, DT8. *Michigan Monument,* Herbert Adams, 1916

The striding, classically draped figure of *Michigan* is cut from the same 40-ton block of Bethel White Granite as the lower third of the obelisk. The carvers achieved a remarkable delicacy in translating the decorative trim from Adams's plaster model of the cloak of *Michigan* to the obdurate stone. The complex curved shapes of the pedestal, cut from another large block of stone, are also notable.

Michigan carries a palm frond symbolic of peace and a gear cog emblematic of industry, which only flourishes in times of peace.

DT9. Dedication of the *Illinois Memorial*
(courtesy Vicksburg National Military Park)

Note the roadway behind the monument in this historic photograph. The road still exists today but is unpaved and grassed over. The names of all 36,325 soldiers from Illinois who served in the campaign and siege are listed on plaques inside the memorial. The structure has a round opening in its roof like the much larger ancient Roman Pantheon that served as the design source for the marble memorial building. The memorial is approached by 47 steps, one for each day of the siege. Note the presence of African Americans along the banks of the road in the foreground—present, but on the periphery of the crowd, as Southern social customs of the times dictated.

DT10. *Illinois Memorial,* **detail of pedimental sculpture, William LeBaron Jenney, architect; Charles Mulligan and Frederick Hibbard, sculptors, 1906**

Charles Mulligan, an instructor at the Chicago Art Institute, made the figurative sculpture depicting *History Recording the Deeds of North and South.* The symbolic pedimental sculpture is crowned by a spread-winged American eagle emblematic of the national unity wrought by the war. The eagle was modeled by another Chicago sculptor, Frederick Hibbard, and cast by a Chicago foundry. It has recently been re-gilded.

DT11. *Gen. John Logan,* **Leonard Crunelle, 1919**

Logan is credited with establishing Memorial Day in the North in May 1866, but memorial services for fallen Confederates predated his efforts by several weeks, and emancipated slaves commemorated those who died in a prisoner-of-war camp in Charleston in the spring of 1865. It is uncontested that North and South alike felt the need to commemorate those who gave their lives in the Civil War. Nearly 25 years passed before the service of survivors began to be memorialized on the battlefield.

DT12. *Wisconsin Monument,* designed by Liance Cottrell, sculpture modeled by Julius Loester, 1911

The *Wisconsin Monument* is topped by a six-foot-tall bronze sculpture of Old Abe, the eagle mascot carried by the Eighth Wisconsin Infantry into 42 battles, including Vicksburg. The present bronze is a replica of the original, which was destroyed by lightning.

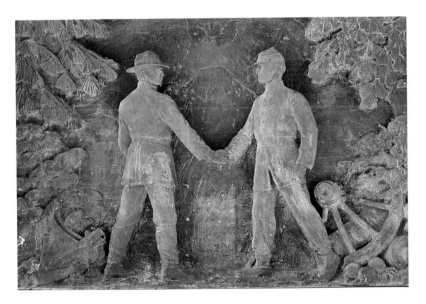

DT13. *Wisconsin Monument,* relief panel on rear of base

On the bas-relief on the rear of the monument a winged female figure hovers above and behind a Union and a Confederate soldier who shake hands amid damaged tools of war. This symbolizes the reconciliation then taking place among the former combatants on the very battlefields where brothers once fought.

DT14. *Wisconsin Monument,* detail of *Infantry*

DT15. *Wisconsin Monument,* detail of *Cavalry*

The coarse cloth of the Wisconsin infantryman's wind-whipped cloak causes dramatic variations in light and shade, thus animating the figure in the Beaux Arts sculptural fashion, but few Union soldiers needed their winter coats in the heat and humidity of the late spring and early summer campaign and siege of Vicksburg.

DT16. Detail of *Eagle* atop the *Kansas Monument,* unknown designer, placed June 1960, no dedication

DT17. *Kansas Monument,* unknown designer, placed June 1960, no dedication

The memorial's three bronze circles—the middle one broken—symbolize the nation before, during, and after the Civil War. An eagle surmounts the *Kansas Monument.*

DT18. *First and Third Mississippi, African Descent,* J. Kim Sessums, 2004

The first and only monument to African Americans on any Civil War battlefield was erected thanks to Robert Walker, the mayor of Vicksburg, who orchestrated an effort to win state grant money to memorialize African American contributions to the campaign and siege of Vicksburg.

DT19. *Rhode Island Monument,* Francis Edwin Elwell, 1908
The dramatic depiction of a color bearer commemorates the single regiment from Rhode Island that served in the campaign and siege of Vicksburg.

DT20. Detail of *Rhode Island Monument*

DT21. *New York Monument*, A. J. Zabriskie, engineer, 1917

The *New York Monument* is exquisitely proportioned and expertly finished. The colossal obelisk, composed of three massive stones, is boldly proportioned. The lower stone of the shaft is roughly surfaced and inset with a bronze state seal and medallions representing the infantry, artillery, and navy. The pedestal sports a dentillated cornice and bronze panels that provide an abundance of historical information but do not distract from the monument's simplicity because each panel reads as a single dark form in contrast with the light stone of the monument. The pedestal is set on a broad base with subtle textual variations and volutes at the four corners. The ensemble sits atop a three-step base with a curved front. The stones are impressive for their sheer size, the small number of stones used, and the precision of their fit.

DT22. *New Hampshire Monument*, **unknown designer, placed 1904, no dedication**
The rough-cut stone from the Granite State is more characteristic of
surface treatments for monuments dating prior to the 1893 "White
City" at Chicago's Columbian Exposition, but the square pillar, capital, and orb finial reflect the popularity of classical architectural forms
after the expo.

DT23. *Massachusetts Monument* (courtesy Vicksburg National Military Park)

DT24, DT25. *Massachusetts Monument,* Theo Alice Ruggles Kitson, 1903

For the first state monument erected in VNMP, Massachusetts shipped an enormous boulder from the state to serve as the pedestal for a duplicate casting of the bronze *Volunteer* that Theo Alice Ruggles Kitson had installed in Newburyport, Massachusetts, in 1902. It took ten yoke of oxen four days to haul the stone from the rail station to its site in the park. Theo's husband Henry supervised the installation because she was home with their second child, who had been born in July. The boulder and bronze were placed on November 13, and the monument was dedicated on the next day before a large crowd that included many veterans from Massachusetts as well as the governor and a large official contingent.

DT26, DT27, DT28. *Pennsylvania Monument,* designed by Albert Ross, architect, sculptural reliefs by Charles Lopez, 1906

The eloquent inscription handsomely engraved on the gracefully curved stele states the monument's purpose succinctly: "Here brothers fought for their principles; here heroes died for their country; and a united people will forever cherish the precious legacy of their noble manhood."

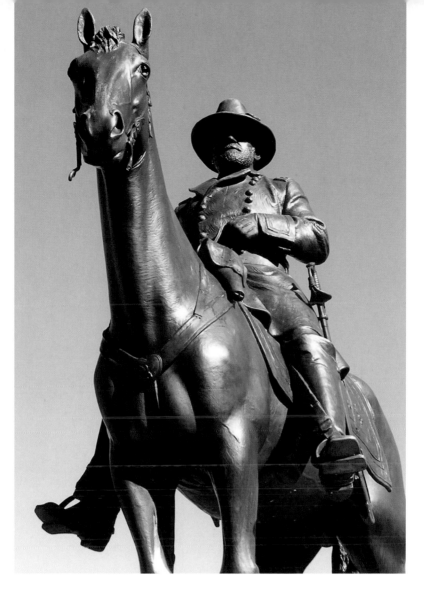

DT29. *Gen. Ulysses Grant,* **Frederick Hibbard, 1918**
This variation on the exedra form of monument (see fig. 4.6) includes
two benches that face the central pedestal supporting the equestrian
portrait of Grant. The design may have been necessitated by the relatively constricted site atop the hill at Grant's headquarters.

DT30. *70th Ohio Monument*
DT31. *Fourth Ohio Battery Monument*

Ohio did not erect a central memorial to all the soldiers and sailors from the state who served at Vicksburg, but it did place monuments for each of the 39 units that fought here. Several are located along this section of Union Avenue.

DT32. *U.S. Navy Memorial,* designer unknown, completed 1911, dedicated 1917
The 202-foot-tall *U.S. Navy Memorial* mimics the design of the 555-foot-tall *Washington Monument* (1858–85) in Washington, D.C., but that memorial is not surrounded by portrait sculptures.

DT33. *Flag Officer Charles Henry Davis,* Francis Elwell, 1910
DT34. *Adm. David D. Porter,* Lorado Taft, 1917
DT35. Detail of *Adm. David Farragut,* Henry Kitson, 1911

DT36. Detail of *Adm. Andrew H. Foote,* William Couper, 1917
DT37. Detail of *Adm. Andrew H. Foote,* William Couper, 1917

DT38. *Lt. Cmdr. Thomas O. Selfridge Jr.*, Henry Kitson, 1913
Selfridge commanded artillery moved from his ships to this location
near the *U.S. Navy Memorial.*

DT39. *National Cemetery Memorial Arch,* designer unknown, date unknown
The *National Cemetery Memorial Arch* is barely visible from the drive
through the cemetery. It is located at the original cemetery entrance
on Washington Street (US 61 BUS). Note the cattle grate and narrow-
gauge dirt track through the arch—vintage features preserved from an
earlier era.

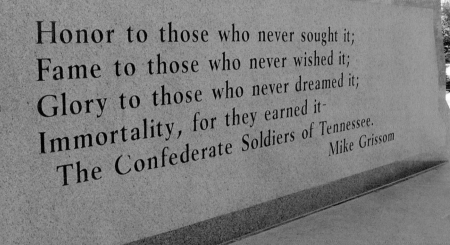

DT40, DT41. *Tennessee Monument,* designer unknown, 1996

DT42. *Missouri Monument,* Victor Holm, 1917
DT43. *The Spirit of the Republic, Missouri Monument,* Victor Holm, 1917

DT44. Detail of Union relief, recently waxed so that it is glossy and readable
DT45. Detail of Confederate relief, unwashed, unwaxed, hard to read

DT46. Detail of top of stele of *Missouri Monument*

DT47. *Missouri Monument* inscription

The *Missouri Monument* sits between the lines where Union and Confederate soldiers from the border state fought. The relief sculptures on the wings of the exedra depict Missouri's Union troops assaulting and Missouri's Confederate troops defending Vicksburg. *The Spirit of the Republic* rides the prow of a battleship beneath the 42-foot-tall stele at the center of the memorial. Missouri sent 42 regiments to the campaign and siege of Vicksburg.

The *Spirit of the Republic,* a modern personification of the ancient Greek *Nike,* or winged Victory figure, carries a fasces—a bundle of rods emblematic of the strength of those rods when joined in union—and holds aloft a sprig of olive, symbolic of peace. More than any other sculpture at VNMP, *The Spirit of the Republic* commemorates the ultimate victory of the Civil War—the reunification of the nation.

DT48, DT49, DT50. *Arkansas Monument,* **designed by William Deacy, architect, sculptor unknown, 1954**

The inscription dedicates the memorial "To the Arkansas Confederate soldiers and sailors, a part of a nation divided by the sword and reunited on the altar of faith." The sword symbolically and physically divides the two halves of the exedra, and its cruciform shape evokes an altar.

DT51. *Surrender Interview Site,* ca. 1906 (courtesy Vicksburg National Military Park)
DT52. *Surrender Interview Site Marker* in 2010

DT53, DT54. *Louisiana Monument,* **Alfred F. Theard, Albert Wieblen Marble and Granite Co., designer, 1920**

The colossal granite Doric column is topped by a tripod with an eternal flame carved in stone. Like the *Louisiana Monument* (DT89) dedicated in 1887 in downtown Vicksburg, it is embellished with the state seal, which features a pelican piercing its own breast to feed its young. The difference in style, scale, and material of the two memorials illustrates the evolution of memorial art and architecture around the turn of the twentieth century. The earlier memorial is small, marble, and dedicated to Louisiana's dead. The later structure is colossal, granite, and dedicated to all Louisianans who served.

DT55, DT56. *Gen. Lloyd Tilghman,* William Seivers, 1926

Gen. Tilghman died at Chestnut Hill on May 16 while protecting the Confederate retreat into Vicksburg. A Union artillery shell nearly cut him in two, but the sculptor portrayed the wound as a small gash in his coat near his heart.

Unlike most equestrian portraits, General Tilghman is shown beside his horse rather than astride it. As with most equestrian monuments, the action and character of the horse contribute to the portrait of the human subject (see also fig. 3.1).

DT57, DT58. *Mississippi Monument,* Frederick Triebel, dedicated 1909, bronze sculpture installed 1912

Clio, the Muse of History, sits enthroned above dramatic depictions of Mississippians defending Vicksburg. She holds a scroll in her lap and may have once held a quill or pen in her right hand. Note the Confederate flag pattern on the fabric band she wears.

Triebel's studio was in Florence, Italy, and he chose a Florentine foundry to cast the memorial's bronze components (as he did for the bronzes on the *Iowa Monument,* dedicated in 1906 at Shiloh). They are the only foreign-made materials in Vicksburg's monuments and memorials. Production delays and customs problems postponed delivery for three years. The many gaps and rough joins between various bronze sections that are evident on close inspection indicate that production standards at the Vignali Foundry did not match those of the American foundries that cast the bronzes on Vicksburg's other memorials.

DT59. *Gen. John Pemberton,* Edmund Quinn, 1917

General Pemberton was virtually disowned by his native state of Pennsylvania for casting his lot with the Confederacy, and he was unpopular throughout the South after the war for not saving Vicksburg. Consequently, VNMP resorted to using federal funds for his portrait, a memorial that pales in comparison with that of his adversary, General Grant (figs. 15.2, DT 29), which was commissioned by Illinois, the state where Grant lived immediately before and after the war.

DT60, DT61. *President Jefferson Davis,* **Henry Kitson, 1927**

Davis hailed from the Vicksburg area, and his brother lived here. Before the war he served as U.S. senator and secretary of war. He holds the Confederate constitution in his right hand and clutches the Confederate flag to his breast. The sculpture was moved from an earlier VNMP visitor center in the 1960s. The Modern-style minimalist brick plaza and benches were added at that time to accommodate the crowds expected for the war's centennial. Unfortunately, the sculpture was resited facing north, perhaps as a symbolic gesture, but it proved to be a monumental faux pas, which makes it difficult to see the front of the figure because the sun is always behind it.

DT62, DT63. *Texas Monument,*
designed by Lundgren and Maurer,
architects, sculpture executed
by Herring Coe, dedicated 1961,
completed 1962–63

This modern classical revival-style exedra faces its Beaux Arts–era predecessor, the *Iowa Monument* (fig. 3.3) across the siege line near the Railroad Redoubt. Both are based on the shape of an ancient Roman bench or seat that became a popular monument form in classical and classical revival art and architecture, but the modern structure's shapes are more simplified than Kitson's early-twentieth-century masterpiece, and there is less sculpture.

DT64, DT65. *Gen. Stephen D. Lee,* Henry Kitson, 1909

General Lee holds the blade of his sword in his gauntleted hand—a detail that evokes his courage and readiness to defend the city. His two-handed grip also enhances his broad shoulders and barrel chest, all of which frame his handsome facial features.

DT64 was made prior to the bronze's cleaning and waxing. DT65 was made after washing and waxing, which restored the jewel-like luster of its surface and protected it from water, which beads on its surface.

DT66. Quarter-scale model for *Alabama Monument* by Steffen Thomas (courtesy Alabama Department of Archives and History)

DT67. Detail of *Alabama Monument*

For additional photographs of the *Alabama Monument* in various stages of design and construction, see figs. 7.1 through 9.3.

The sculptor offered this "Interpretation of the Alabama Memorial" in his book, *Sculpture by Steffen Thomas* (1951):

This flag is the spirit of Alabama which never fell, being upheld and defended by men and women alike. The woman represents the womanhood of Alabama who stood ever ready to give comfort spiritually as well as physically—who maintained the home and with her courage supported the courage of her men, and with her inspiration kept forever high the spirit of Alabama against all odds—who long after the war staunchly nurtured the flame that was the beautiful life and ideal of the South—and through the endurance of physical hardships and cloudiness of long years has not let it die even to this day—this woman is Alabama herself. These men are the heroes who, with the last vestige of physical and moral courage, took a death stand in defense of their Southern ideals, their homes, the womanhood, and the spirit of Alabama.

DT68. *Kentucky Confederate Monument,* 2010
DT69. *Georgia Monument,* designed by Harry Sellers, Marietta Memorials, 1962
Georgia's Vicksburg monument is identical in design to contemporaneous Georgia monuments at Gettysburg and Antietam. Unlike other state memorials at Vicksburg that commemorate veterans as well as the fallen, Georgia's is inscribed in honor of its dead: "We sleep here in obedience to law; When duty called, we came; When country called, we died."

DT70. *VNMP Commissioner William T. Rigby,* Henry Kitson, 1928, with Iowa
regimental monument

DT71. Dedication of *Kentucky Monument,* Terry Lovejoy, Muldoon Memorials, designer, Gary Casteel, sculptor, 2001 (courtesy Vicksburg National Military Park)

DT72. Detail of *Kentucky Monument,* Terry Lovejoy, Muldoon Memorials, designer, Gary Casteel, sculptor, 2001

Presidents Lincoln and Davis never met on the battlefield, but both were born in Kentucky. Early designs showed them shaking hands, but that was thought to be too confusing for viewers. The life-sized bronzes were originally placed about six feet apart, facing east, but were reset shortly after the dedication.

Other bronze figures at VNMP are heroic in scale—larger than life, as is appropriate for the subjects' heroic actions—and raised on pedestals rather than set on the low plinth that permits viewers to stand with the sculptures, a design feature of many public sculptures in the United States in the late twentieth century, when artists created works that merged art with its audience rather than setting sculptures above and beyond the living. Consequently, these sculptures lack the commanding presence of Vicksburg's earlier portrait figures.

DT73. *Iowa Monument,* **designed and executed by Henry Kitson with the assistance of his wife, Theo Alice Ruggles Kitson, and architect Guy Lowell, dedicated 1906; bronze equestrian color bearer installed 1912**

Henry Hudson Kitson and his wife Theo Alice Ruggles Kitson created the *Iowa Monument,* the *Massachusetts Monument,* 3 portrait figures, 24 portrait busts, and 54 portrait reliefs at Vicksburg, far more than any other pair of artists at Vicksburg. Still, their Vicksburg memorials represent a small portion of their lifetime production.

The six relief panels on this monument exhibit some of the highest relief sculpture found on any Civil War battlefield. The upper portions of some of the figures are modeled in three dimensions, fully free from the background plane of the relief. In order to meet the tight timetable for delivery of the reliefs prior to the dedication, Kitson employed three different foundries (Roman Bronze, Bureau Brothers, and Gorham). Unfortunately, some of the stone had to be trimmed to install the reliefs.

DT74. *Iowa Monument,* **detail of** *Flagbearer*

The equestrian flag-bearer was not in place when the monument was dedicated. Its production was delayed due to Henry Kitson's illness. Theo was subsequently responsible for so much of its creation from Henry's small model that he credited her with the sculpture. Consequently, this may be the first monumental equestrian sculpture by a female artist.

This photo of the recently cleaned and waxed bronze reveals the dark, glossy, jewel-like character the bronze had when it was new. Details like the stars and stripes are visible, as are faint green stains where casting flaws are accelerating corrosion.

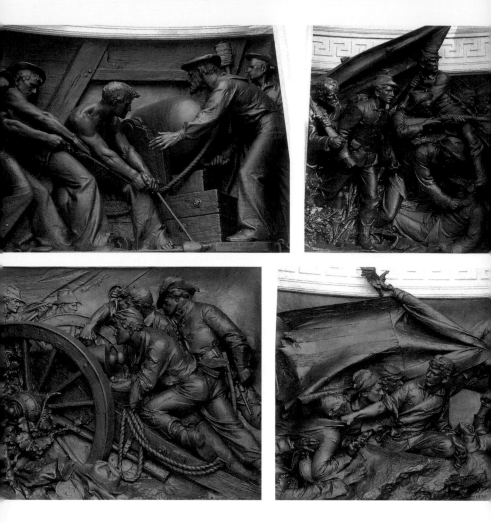

DT75, DT76, DT77, DT78. *Iowa Monument* reliefs

DT79. *Maj. Gen. O. C. Ord,* Anton
Schaaf, 1916
DT80. *Gen. John McClernand,* Edward
Potter, 1919

Potter was renowned for his
facility with horses and other animals. He made the mounts for
several equestrian monuments
commissioned from Daniel
Chester French, the sculptor of
the colossal *Lincoln* in the *Lincoln
Memorial* in Washington, D.C.
Potter also made the beloved lions on the steps of the New York
Public Library.

Notice how McClernand's atten-
tive horse twists one ear forward
and one ear to the rear. Note how that affects one's observation of the
sculpture as the viewer moves from the horse's front to his right side.

DT81. *Lt. Col. William Vilas,* **A. A. Weinman, 1912**

Weinman conceived this monument and won the commission, hiring an architect to assist with architectural and construction details. The results speak volumes about the high quality of monument design and construction in America in the early twentieth century. Simplicity and attention to detail proved to be key criteria employed by these exemplary professionals in the integration of this magnificent portrait with its carefully proportioned pedestal and plaza (see also figs. 11.2, 16.2, 16.3, 16.4).

DT82. *Monument to the Confederate Dead,* designer unknown, 1892, Cedar Hill
  Cemetery, Vicksburg

The stone sentinel standing at Parade Rest over the graves of many
Southerners who died in the campaign and siege of Vicksburg is more
typical of the quiet and contemplative statuary erected in both the
North and South in cemeteries and civic settings such as county courthouse lawns than it is of the active soldier statues favored by patrons
of Civil War battlefield memorials.

DT83. *North Carolina Monument,* Weiblen Marble and Granite Works, 1925
DT84. *Florida Monument,* designer unknown, 1954

The North Carolina and Florida monuments commemorate soldiers in Gen. Joseph E. Johnston's Army of Relief.

DT85. *Maryland Monument,* designer unknown, 1914

Third Maryland Battery, CSA, Monument and the *South Carolina Monument* were both erected with private funds.

DT86. *South Carolina Monument,* **designer unknown, 1935**
Subtle streamlined design features characteristic of the Art Deco style popular in the 1930s are evident in this granite stele, especially on the top of this simple and relatively inexpensive memorial.

DT87, DT88. *Virginia Monument,* **designer unknown, 1907**
The *Virginia Monument* commemorates the Botetourt Artillery, the only Virginia unit to serve in the campaign and siege of Vicksburg. Its site by a busy intersection cluttered with signage and utility poles is a stark contrast to the quiet roads inside VNMP, which are restricted to tourist traffic.

DT89. *Louisiana Monument,* **designer unknown, 1887**

This marble monument was erected a dozen years before VNMP was established, and was located near the center of town. The state seal features a pelican piercing its own breast to feed its young—a vivid emblem of self-sacrifice that is especially appropriate for a war memorial. Like many Civil War memorials dedicated nationwide in the twenty-five years following the war, it is dedicated to those who died, not to all those who served.

DT90, DT91. *Connecticut Monument,*
Mathieu Memorial and Granite Works,
with the assistance of Kerry Shelden
for digital designs, 2008

A map of Connecticut is visible in
the stained concrete in the middle
of the plaza adjacent to the site of
Grant's unfinished canal. Canal
construction was started in an attempt to circumnavigate Vicksburg's batteries in the summer of
1862, but the heat, humidity, and
swampy conditions resulted in the
deaths of 150 men of the Ninth
Connecticut before the effort was
abandoned.

For more information about
how this twenty-first-century monument was designed and fabricated, please see Chapter 10.

20 Comprehensive List of Major Group Memorials and All Portrait Memorials on the Driving Tour

Major group memorials, equestrian portraits, portrait figures, busts, and reliefs are listed in the order they are encountered along the 16-mile VNMP tour route. Directions are also provided for the memorials sited outside the park boundaries.

To locate a specific group monument or portrait, please see the index.

Generally, the name of a monument's subject is followed by its date of dedication, the name of the sculptor or designer, and the name of the foundry or fabricator.

Surrender Interview Site Monument, erected by Union Troops July 4, 1864, on the site of the interview, currently located inside the VNMP Visitor Center (GPS 32.34407 -90.85153)

North Loop, Union Avenue

Memorial Arch erected spanning Clay Street in 1920; moved into park in 1967; Charles Lawhon, architect (GPS 32.34373 -90.84936)

Brig. Gen. Stephen G. Burbridge bust, date unknown; T. A. R. Kitson, Gorham Co.

Col. William J. Landram relief, 1914; Victor Holm, Jules Berchem

Col. Jesse I. Alexander, 1918 relief; T. A. R. Kitson, Gorham Co.

Minnesota Monument, May 24, 1907; William Couper, sculptor, Gorham Co. (GPS 32.35000 -90.84529)

Col. John B. Sanborn bust, 1914; T. A. R. Kitson, Gorham Co.

Col. Green B. Raum relief, 1915; George E. Ganiere, Jules Berchem

Col. Samuel L. Holmes relief, 1915; T. A. R. Kitson, Gorham Co.

Col. George B. Boomer relief, T. A. R. Kitson, Tiffany Studios

Brig. Gen. Isaac F. Quinby bust, 1911; William Couper, Roman Bronze Works

Brig. Gen. Charles L. Matthies relief, 1913; T. A. R. Kitson, Gorham Co.

Col. Holden Putnam relief, 1919; T. A. R. Kitson, Gorham Co.

Pemberton Avenue intersects on left; continue straight on Union Avenue.

Michigan Monument, Nov. 10, 1916; Herbert Adams, sculptor
(GPS 32.35380 -90.84114)

Gen. John Logan Monument, 1919; Leonard Crunelle, American
Art Bronze (GPS 32.35916 -90.83968)

Brig. Gen. John E. Smith bust, 1919; George E. Ganiere, American
Art Bronze

Col. Manning Force relief, 1912; T. A. R. Kitson, Gorham Co.

Illinois Memorial, October 26, 1906; William B. Jenney, architect, Charles J. Mulligan and Frederick C. Hibbard, sculptors;
three relief portraits under portico of Illinois Memorial (GPS
32.35975 -90.84149)

> *President Abraham Lincoln* bust, Charles J. Mulligan,
> sculptor
> *Gen. U. S. Grant* bust, Charles J. Mulligan, sculptor
> *Illinois Governor Richard Yates* bust, Charles J. Mulligan,
> sculptor

Brig. Gen. Mortimer D. Leggett relief, 1911; Henry Kitson, Tiffany
Studios

Capt. Andrew Hickenlooper Monument, 1912; William Couper,
Jno. Williams Fdry. (GPS 32.35878 -90.84375)

Park and walk on the unpaved service road leading toward Louisiana
Redan to see the next three portrait reliefs.

Lt. Col. Melancthon Smith relief, 1916; George T. Brewster, Gorham Co.

Col. Eugene Erwin relief, CSA, 1916; George T. Brewster, Gorham
Co.

Lt. Col. Pembroke S. Senteny relief, CSA, 1920; T. A. R. Kitson, Gorham Co.

Proceed driving on Union Avenue north of the *Illinois Memorial.*

Brig. Gen. John McArthur bust, 1919; George E. Ganiere, American
Art Bronze

Brig. Gen. Thomas E. G. Ransom bust, 1916; George T. Brewster,
Gorham Co.

Wisconsin Monument, May 22, 1911; Liance Cottrell, designer and
architect, Julius C. Loester, sculptor, Roman Bronze Works,
foundry (GPS 32.36531 -90.84037)

Brig. Gen. Marcellus M. Crocker bust, 1913; T. A. R. Kitson, Gorham Co.

Col. Alexander Chambers relief, 1918; T. A. R. Kitson, Gorham Co.

Col. William Hall relief, 1915; T. A. R. Kitson, Gorham Co.

Brig. Gen. Giles A. Smith bust, 1913; Solon H. Borglum, Roman Bronze Works

West Virginia Monument/Maj. Arza M. Goodspeed, November 14, 1922; Aristride Berto Cianfarani, Gorham Co. (GPS 32.36987 -90.8404)

Brig. Gen. Hugh Ewing relief, 1911; T. A. R. Kitson, Gorham Co.

Col. Joseph R. Cockerill relief, 1918; T. A. R. Kitson, Gorham Co.

Maj. Gen. Francis P. Blair, Jr. relief, 1911; William Couper, Roman Bronze Works

Graveyard Road intersects from the left; continue straight on Grant Avenue.

Union Avenue turns left; continue straight on Grant Avenue.

Brig. Gen. Cadwallader C. Washburne Monument, 1919; George T. Brewster, Gorham Co. (GPS 32.37466 -90.83819)

Sherman Circle intersects on the left; continue straight on Grant Avenue.

Col. Milton Montgomery relief, 1913; T. A. R. Kitson, Gorham Co.

Col. George W. Neely relief, 1916; Roland Hinton Perry, Gorham Co.

Brig. Gen. Elias S. Dennis bust, 1915; George T. Brewster, Gorham Co.

Col. Isaac F. Shepard relief, 1916; Roland Hinton Perry, Gorham Co.

Brig. Gen. Hugh T. Reid relief, 1915; Anton Schaaf, Jno. Williams Fdry.

Kansas Monument, placed June 1960, no dedication; unknown designer (GPS 32.37436 -90.83382)

First and Third Mississippi, African Descent Monument, dedicated February 14, 2004; J. Kim Sessums, sculptor, Weston Studio Foundry (GPS 32.37396 -90.83330)

Col. Cyrus Bussy relief, 1911; Francis E. Elwell, Jno. Williams Fdry.

Brig. Gen. Robert B. Potter bust, 1914; Roland Hinton Perry, no foundry mark

Brig. Gen. William Sooy Smith bust, 1913; Solon H. Borglum, A. Griffout & Brothers

Gen. Nathan Kimball bust, 1915; George T. Brewster, Gorham Co.

Brig. Gen. Edward Ferrero bust, 1915; T. A. R. Kitson, Gorham Co.

Capt. Cyrus B. Comstock, 1910; T. A. R. Kitson, Tiffany Studios

Rhode Island Monument, November 11, 1908; Francis Edwin El-
well, sculptor (GPS 32.37602 -90.83239)
Col. William W. Sanford relief, 1918; T. A. R. Kitson, Gorham Co.
Capt. Frederick Prime relief, 1911; T. A. R. Kitson, Gorham Co.
Lt. James H. Wilson relief, 1910; T. A. R. Kitson, Tiffany Studios
New York Monument, October 17, 1917; A. J. Zabriskie (GPS
32.37629 -90.83344)
Lt. Col. John A. Rawlins relief, 1911; T. A. R. Kitson, Tiffany
Studios
Massachusetts Monument, November 14, 1903; Theo Alice Rug-
gles Kitson, sculptor (GPS 32.37708 -90.83325)
Col. Simon G. Griffin relief, 1915; Anton Schaaf, Jno. Williams Fdry.
New Hampshire Monument, placed November 1904, no dedica-
tion; unknown designer (GPS 32.37717 -90.8336)
Brig. Gen. Thomas Welsh bust, 1913; Roland Hinton Perry, no
foundry mark
Pennsylvania Governor Andrew G. Curtin bust, 1930; R. Tait Mc
Kenzie, no foundry mark
Maj. Gen. John Grubb Parke bust, 1930; R. Tait McKenzie, no
foundry mark
Pennsylvania Memorial, March 24, 1906; Albert Randolph Ross,
architect, Charles Lopez, sculptor of portrait reliefs (GPS
32.37792 -90.83361)
    Col. John I. Curtin relief
    Lt. Col. Thomas S. Brenholtz relief
    Col. John F. Hartranft relief
    Col. Daniel Leasure relief
    Capt. George W. Durell relief
Gen. Ulysses S. Grant Monument, 1918; Frederick Hibbard, Florentine Brotherhood Foundry (GPS 32.37717 -90.83440)

Turn right on Sherman Avenue.

Col. John M. Loomis relief, 1918, T. A. R. Kitson, Gorham Co.

Turn right on Grant Avenue, then right on North Union Avenue, toward
Cairo Museum.

Brig. Gen. James W. Tuttle bust, 1912; T. A. R. Kitson, Gorham Co.
Brig. Gen. Ralph P. Buckland bust, 1915; Henry Kitson, possibly
American Art Bronze
Col. William L. McMillen bust, 1915; T. A. R. Kitson, Gorham Co.

Maj. Gustavus Lightfoot, 1914; Henry Kitson, Tiffany Studios

Col. Adolph Engelmann relief, 1916; Bruce W. Saville, Gorham Co.

Brig. Gen. John M. Thayer bust, 1915; T. A. R. Kitson, Gorham Co.

Col. Bernard G. Farrar relief, 1914; George E. Ganiere, Jules Berchem

Col. Francis H. Manter relief, 1915; Victor S. Holm, Alloyed Metal & Mfg. Co.

Col. Jonathan Richmond relief, 1916; Bruce W. Saville, Gorham Co.

U.S. Navy Memorial, completed 1911, dedicated October 17, 1917; designer unknown (GPS 32.37644 -90.86403)

    Adm. David Farragut statue, 1911; Henry Kitson, Tiffany Studios

    Adm. David D. Porter statue, 1917; Lorado Taft, American Art Bronze

    Flag Officer Charles Henry Davis statue, 1910; Francis E. El well, Gorham Co.

    Adm. Andrew H. Foote statue, 1917; William Couper, Gorham Co.

Lt. Cmdr. Thomas O. Selfridge bust, Jr., 1913; Henry Kitson, Gorham Co.

Brig. Gen. Alfred W. Ellet bust, 1915; T. A. R. Kitson, Tiffany Studios

Col. Charles R. Woods bust, 1912; T. A. R. Kitson, probably Tiffany Studios

Maj. Gen. Frederick Steele Monument, 1912; Francis Edwin Elwell, Gorham Co. (GPS 32.37474 -90.86648)

Cairo Museum and Vicksburg National Cemetery

National Cemetery Memorial Arch is barely visible from the drive through the cemetery but is accessible by a short walk from the tour route. It is located in the southwest corner of the cemetery, at the original entrance on Washington Street/U.S. 61 BUS. Parking is easier inside the cemetery than on Washington Street. (GPS 32.37337 -90.87097)

Confederate Avenue, North Loop

Brig. Gen. Jeptha V. Harris, CSA, relief, 1915; George E. Ganiere, Jules Berchem

Brig. Gen. John C. Vaughn, CSA, relief, 1911; T. A. R. Kitson, Tiffany Studios

Tennessee Monument, June 29, 1996; unknown designer (GPS 32.37154 -90.86198)

Brig. Gen. John Adams, CSA, bust, 1915; Anton Schaaf, Jno. Williams Fdry.

Col. Randall MacGavock, CSA, relief, 1919; George T. Brewster, Gorham Co.

Brig. Gen. William E. Baldwin, CSA, bust, 1915; T. A. R. Kitson, Gorham Co.

Lt. Col. Madison Rogers, CSA, relief, 1919; George T. Brewster, Gorham Co.

Lt. Col. Sidney H. Griffin, CSA, relief, 1919; George T. Brewster, Gorham Co.

Col. Robert Richardson, CSA, relief, 1910; T. A. R. Kitson, Tiffany Studios

Maj. William W. Martin, CSA, relief, 1911; T. A. R. Kitson, Tiffany Studios

Capt. Lewis Guion, CSA, relief, 1920; T. A. R. Kitson, Gorham Co.

Brig. Gen. Francis S. Shoup, CSA, 1910; T. A. R. Kitson, Tiffany Studios

Col. Allen Thomas, CSA, relief, 1910; T. A. R. Kitson, Tiffany Studios

Maj. Gen. John S. Bowen, CSA, bust, 1916; Anton Schaaf, no foundry mark

Col. William Wade, CSA, relief, 1912; Francis E. Elwell, Jno. Williams Fdry.

Maj. Gen. Martin L. Smith, CSA, bust, 1911; Henry Kitson, Roman Bronze Works

Col. Francis M. Cockrell, CSA, relief, 1915; Allen G. Newman, sculptor and founder

Col. Leon D. Marks, CSA, 1910; relief, T. A. R. Kitson, Tiffany Studios

Lt. Col. Lauren L. McLauren, CSA, relief, 1921; George T. Brewster, Gorham Co.

Turn left on Graveyard Road to see the following six portrait reliefs. CAUTION!

This route will require driving along North Union Avenue to the Cairo Museum and then on North Confederate Avenue to return to this point on the tour.

Capt. Edward C. Washington relief, 1910; T. A. R. Kitson, Tiffany Studios

Brig. Gen. Joseph Mower relief, 1911; Solon H. Borglum, no foundry mark

Col. Thomas K. Smith relief, 1912; Louis Milione, Bureau Brothers

Capt. William Jenney relief, 1911; T. A. R. Kitson, Tiffany Studios

Brig. Gen. Joseph A. J. Lightburn relief, 1915; Victor S. Holm, Jules Berchem

Col. Joseph J. Woods relief, 1910; T. A. R. Kitson, Tiffany Studios

Return to Confederate Avenue, North Loop, at Graveyard Road; continue on Confederate Avenue.

Maj. Alexander Yates, CSA, relief, 1917; George T. Brewster, Gorham Co.

Col. Thomas P. Dockery, CSA, relief, 1915; Victor S. Holm, Jules Berchem

Brig. Gen. Martin E. Green, CSA, relief, 1911; T. A. R. Kitson, Tiffany Studios

Missouri Monument, October 17, 1917; Victor S. Holm, sculptor, Hellmuth and Hellmuth, architects (GPS 32.36849 -90.84472)

Arkansas Monument, August 2, 1954; William Henry Deacy, designer (GPS 32.36857 -90.84565)

Col. James Henry Jones, CSA, relief, 1912; T. A. R. Kitson, Tiffany Studios

Turn left on Pemberton Avenue.

Surrender Interview Site Marker (GPS 32.35745 -90.84463)

Brig. Gen. John D. Stevenson relief, 1911; T. A. R. Kitson, Tiffany Studios

At old VNMP administration building, reverse direction and return to Confederate Avenue, North Loop, then turn left.

Brig. Gen. Louis Hebert, CSA, relief, 1910; T. A. R. Kitson, Tiffany Studios

Louisiana Monument, October 18, 1920; Alfred Iheard, Albert Wieblen Marble and Granite Co., designer (GPS 32.35712 -90.84700)

Brig. Gen. Daniel W. Adams, CSA, bust, 1912; T. A. R. Kitson, possibly cast by Tiffany Studios

Gen. Lloyd Tilghman, CSA, monument, 1926; William Sievers, Gorham Co. (GPS 32.35692 -90.8485)

Col. William W. Witherspoon, CSA, relief, 1915; George E. Ganiere, Jules Berchem

Maj. Gen. John H. Forney, CSA, monument, 1951; Steffen Thomas, Modern Art Foundry

Maj. Samuel H. Lockett, CSA, relief, 1911; T. A. R. Kitson, Tiffany Studios

Mississippi Monument, dedicated November 13, 1909, completed 1912; Frederick E. Triebel, designer and sculptor, G. Vignali, foundry (GPS 32.35296 -90.85175)

Gen. John Pemberton, CSA, monument, 1917; Edmund Quinn,
Roman Bronze Works (GPS 32.35172 -90.85220)

Maj. Robert Campbell, CSA, relief, 1920; George T. Brewster,
Gorham Co.

Maj. Gen. Dabney H. Maury, CSA, bust, 1915; George T. Brewster,
Gorham Co.

Col. William T. Withers, CSA, bust, 1929; Albert G. Rieker, Roman
Bronze Works

President Jefferson Davis Monument 1927; Henry Kitson, no
foundry mark (GPS 32.34731 -90.85462)

Brig. Gen. John C. Moore, CSA, relief, 1911; T. A. R. Kitson, Tiffany
Studios

Capt. Patrick H. White relief, 1917; George T. Brewster, Gorham Co.

Col. Thomas J. Lucas relief, 1916; Allen G. Newman, sculptor and
founder

Lt. Peter C. Hains relief, 1910; T. A. R. Kitson, Tiffany Studios

Turn right to Confederate Avenue, South Loop.

Texas Monument, dedicated November 4, 1961, completed 1962–
63; Lundgren and Maurer, architects, Herring Coe, sculptor
(GPS 32.34290 -90.85629)

Col. Thomas N. Waul, CSA, bust, 1912; T. A. R. Kitson, Gorham Co.

Gen. Stephen D. Lee, CSA, monument, 1909; Henry H. Kitson,
Roman Bronze Works (GPS 32.34223 -90.85789)

Alabama Monument, July 19, 1951; Steffen Thomas, sculptor,
Modern Art Foundry (GPS 32.33967 -90.85952)

Kentucky Confederate Monument, dedicated May 8, 2010 (GPS
32.33814 -90.86030)

Brig. Gen. Edward D. Tracy, CSA, bust, 1913; Solon H. Borglum,
Roman Bronze Works

Brig. Gen. Isham W. Garrott, CSA, bust, 1909; William Couper,
Gorham Co.

Georgia Monument, October 25, 1962; Harry Sellers, designer,
Marietta Memorials, fabricator (GPS 32.33601 -90.86348)

Confederate Avenue becomes Union Avenue, South Loop.

Brig. Gen. George F. McGinnis relief, 1911; T. A. R. Kitson, Tiffany
Studios

Indiana Governor Oliver Perry Morton Monument, June 16, 1926;
George T. Brewster, Gorham Co. (GPS 32.3328 -90.8626)

Brig. Gen. Alvin P. Hovey bust, 1915; George T. Brewster, Gorham Co.

VNMP Commission Chairman Capt. William Rigby bust, 1928; Henry Kitson, Roman Bronze Works (GPS 32.33509 -90.86005)

Col. James R. Slack relief, 1912; Adolph A. Weinman, Gorham Co.

Park and walk on the *Kentucky Monument* access path; no vehicular access.

Brig. Gen. Benjamin H. Helm, CSA, bust, 1914; Anton Schaaf, Jno. Williams Fdry.

Brig. Gen. Jacob Lauman bust, 1914; Roland Hinton Perry, Laser and Co.

Brig. Gen. William Vandiver bust, 1915; George T. Brewster, Gorham Co.

Maj. Gen. John C. Breckinridge, CSA, bust, 1913; T. A. R. Kitson, Gorham Co.

Kentucky Monument, October 20, 2001; Terry Joy, designer (GPS 32.33705 -90.86027)

   C.S.A. Pres. Jefferson Davis statue, Gary Casteel, sculptor
   U.S. Pres. Abraham Lincoln statue, Gary Casteel, sculptor
   Brig. Gen. George B. Cosby, CSA, bust, 1915; Anton Schaaf, Jno. Williams Fdry.

Continue driving on Union Avenue, South Loop, beyond the *Kentucky Monument* access path.

Brig. Gen. Theophilus T. Garrard relief, 1912; T. A. R. Kitson, Tiffany Studios

Col. James Keigwin relief, 1914; T. A. R. Kitson, Gorham Co.

Col. Daniel W. Lindsey relief, 1915; T. A. R. Kitson, Gorham Co.

Brig. Gen. Peter J. Osterhaus bust, 1913; T. A. R. Kitson, Gorham Co.

Col. Lionel A. Sheldon relief, 1914; Victor S. Holm, Jules Berchem

Iowa Governor Samuel J. Kirkwood bust, 1927; Henry Kitson, American Art Foundry

Iowa Monument, dedicated November 15, 1906, completed 1912; Henry Hudson Kitson, designer and sculptor (with equestrian sculpture assistance from Theo Alice Ruggles Kitson), Guy Lowell, architect (GPS 32.33911 -90.85298)

Maj. Gen. Edward O. C. Ord Monument, 1916; Anton Schaaf, Jno. Williams Fdry. (GPS 32.33970 -90.85279)

Gen. John McClernand Monument, 1919, Edward Potter, Gorham Co. (GPS 32.33989 -90.85273)

Brig. Gen. Michael Lawler bust, 1915; Anton Schaaf, Jno. Williams Fdry.

Col. Charles L. Harris relief, 1913; T. A. R. Kitson, Gorham Co.

Col. Henry D. Washburn relief, 1915; T. A. R. Kitson, Gorham Co.

Brig. Gen. Eugene A. Carr, 1916; Roland Hinton Perry, Gorham Co.

Brig. Gen. William P. Benton relief, 1911; T. A. R. Kitson, Tiffany Studios

Col. David Shunk relief, 1915; Victor S. Holm, Jules Berchem

Col. William Vilas Monument, 1912; Adolph Alexander Weinman, Gorham Co. (GPS 32.34437 -90.85225)

CAUTION!

The monuments and memorials listed below are sited along public roads, many of which are narrow, curved, and carry heavy local traffic. There are few roadside parking areas. Please obey all traffic laws, drive defensively, and respect private property.

From VNMP Visitor Center, turn right on Clay Street.

Maj. Gen. Andrew J. Smith bust, 1911; Francis E. Elwell, Gorham Co. (across Clay Street from entrance to VNMP)

Maj. Gen. William H. T. Walker, CSA, bust, 1913; T. A. R. Kitson, Gorham Co. (north side of Clay Street at Melborn Place)

Turn left on Melborn Place.

Brig. Gen. John Gregg, CSA, bust, 1914; Solon H. Borglum, Roman Bronze Works

Brig. Gen. Matthew D. Ector, CSA, bust, 1915; Anton Schaaf, Jno. Williams Fdry.

Return to Clay Street and turn left, proceed one half mile to Mission 66 Road and turn right.

Proceed past Martin Luther King, Jr. Boulevard to Sky Farm Road and turn right, then enter Cedar Hills Cemetery on the left. Proceed straight to the Civil War section of the cemetery.

Monument to the Confederate Dead, artist unknown, 1892, Cedar Hill Cemetery, Vicksburg (GPS 32.36638 -90.85948)

Return to Sky Farm Avenue and turn right. Then turn left on Mission 66 Road. At Clay Street, turn right and proceed one mile to Monroe Street and turn left.

Louisiana Monument, 1887; unknown designer (GPS 32.34855 -90.87999)

Return to Clay Street and turn right. After one mile turn right on Mission 66 Road, which soon widens into South Confederate Avenue.

> *Brig. Gen. Alfred Cumming, CSA,* relief, 1911; T. A. R. Kitson, Tiffany Studios (100 yards south of Indiana Avenue.)

Turn left on Wisconsin Avenue.

> *Col. Issac C. Pugh* relief, 1916; T. A. R. Kitson, Gorham Co. (about 350 yards south of South Confederate Avenue, at intersection with Autumn Drive)

Return to South Confederate Avenue and turn left.

> *Brig. Gen. Thomas H. Taylor, CSA,* bust 1915; T. A. R. Kitson, Gorham Co.
> *Brig. Gen. Marcellus A. Stovall, CSA,* bust, 1915; T. A. R. Kitson, Gorham Co.
> *Col. Claudius C. Wilson, CSA,* relief, 1915; T. A. R. Kitson, Gorham Co.

Turn left on Halls Ferry Road.

> *Col. Cyrus Hall* relief, 1915; Anton Schaaf, Jno. Williams Fdry. (280 yards south of South Confederate Avenue overpass)
> *Col. George E. Bryant* relief, 1913; T. A. R. Kitson, Gorham Co. (100 yards south of Salient Works)
> *Col. Amory K. Johnson* relief, 1915; George E. Ganiere, Jules Berchem (450 yards south of Confederate Avenue overpass)

Return to South Confederate Avenue and turn left.

> *Maj. Gen. Carter L. Stevenson, CSA,* bust, 1914; T. A. R. Kitson, Gorham Co.
> *Maj. Joseph W. Anderson, CSA,* relief, 1919; George T. Brewster, Gorham Co.
> *North Carolina Monument,* 1925; Albert Wieblen, designer, Aristide Berto Cianfarani, sculptor (GPS 32.32837 -90.87818)

Intersect Mulvihill Road. Continue straight on South Confederate Avenue.

> *Florida Monument,* 1954; unknown designer (GPS 32.32707 -90.88043)

Col. Alexander W. Reynolds, CSA, relief, 1911; T. A. R. Kitson,
Tiffany Studios

Brig. Gen. Abraham Buford, CSA, relief, 1911; T. A. R. Kitson,
Tiffany Studios

Maj. Gen. William W. Loring, CSA, bust, 1911; T. A. R. Kitson,
Tiffany Studios

Maryland Monument, 1914; designer unknown (GPS 32.3248
-90.88188)

Col. Arthur E. Reynolds, CSA, relief, 1915; George E. Ganiere,
Jules Berchem

Brig. Gen. Winfield S. Featherston, CSA, bust, 1915; Edmond T.
Quinn, Roman Bronze Works

Brig. Gen. States Rights Gist, CSA, bust, 1915; George T. Brewster,
Gorham Co.

Pass Vicksburg High School.

South Carolina Monument, 1935, unknown designer (GPS
32.32099 -90.88534)

Brig. Gen. Nathan G. Evans, CSA, bust, 1914; Louis Milione,
no foundry mark

Col. Skidmore Harris, CSA, relief, 1919; George T. Brewster,
Gorham Co. (200 yards north of Frontage Road)

Brig. Gen. Seth M. Barton, CSA, relief, 1911; T. A. R. Kitson,
Tiffany Studios (200 yards north of Frontage Road)

Lt. Francis Obenchain, CSA, bust, 1927; Frederick Hibbard,
Chicago Art Bronze Works

Turn right on N. I-20 Frontage Road.

Virginia Monument, 1907; unknown designer (at the intersection
with Iowa Avenue) (GPS 32.31773 -90.88940)

Brig. Gen. Evander McNair, CSA, bust, 1915; Anton Schaaf,
Jno. Williams Fdry.

Maj. Gen. Samuel G. French, CSA, bust, 1914; Roland Hinton Perry, no foundry mark

Brig. Gen. Samuel B. Maxey, CSA, bust, 1915; T. A. R. Kitson,
Gorham Co.

Cross long bridge over Stouts Bayou and railroad tracks.

Col. Lawrence S. Ross, CSA, relief, 1915; Anton Schaaf,
Jno. Williams Fdry. (100 yards west of long bridge)

Brig. Gen. John W. Whitfield, CSA, bust, 1913; George T. Brewster, Gorham Co. (on left at intersection with Washington Street)

Brig. Gen. William H. "Red" Jackson, CSA, bust, 1913; Roland Hinton Perry, no foundry mark (on right at intersection with Washington Street)

Turn right on Washington Street, US 61 BUS, then turn left on Louisiana Circle.

Louisiana Circle (Mississippi River Overlook) (GPS 32.31966 -90.89697)

Capt. Toby Hart, CSA, relief, 1921; George T. Brewster, Gorham Co.

Col. Edward Higgins, CSA, relief, 1910; T. A. R. Kitson, Tiffany Studios

Maj. Frederick N. Ogden, CSA, relief, 1921; George T. Brewster, Gorham Co.

Turn right on Washington Street.

There are no portraits at South Fort (GPS 32.31587 -90.89834) or Navy Circle (GPS 32.31263 -90.89997), but other memorials are located there.

At Exit 1A, take I-20 West, cross the Mississippi River and proceed three miles to the first exit (Exit 186), turn right, then turn right on old U.S. 80 and proceed toward Delta, MS, to Grant's Canal Reservation of VNMP (on the right, drive under I-20).

Connecticut Monument, October 14, 2008; Mathieu Memorial and Granite Works, with the assistance of Kerry Shelden on digital designs (GPS 32.32065 -90.93278)

Return to I-20, Exit 186, via old U.S. 80; go east on I-20 across the Mississippi River to Exit 1-C. Turn right on Halls Ferry Road, then take the first right on Pemberton Square Boulevard.

The memorials to Brig. Gen. Orme and Maj. Gen. Herron are among a group of monuments on the left side of the road (GPS 32.31437 -90.88007).

Brig. Gen. William W. Orme, CSA, relief, 1917; T. A. R. Kitson, Gorham Co.

Maj. Gen. Francis J. Herron relief, 1914; Solon H. Borglum, Roman Bronze Works

The last portrait on the driving tour is located about six miles from this point, just north of VNMP.

Col. Stephen G. Hicks relief, 1915; Bruce W. Saville, Gorham Co.

It is located at the intersection of Sherman Avenue and Short Sherman Avenue, which was once an access route to VNMP at Sherman Circle (GPS 32.38037 -90.83852).

It can be reached by taking I-20 East to U.S. 61 North (exit 5), then turning left at Sherman Avenue Elementary School (across U.S. 61 from River Region Medical Center), then right on Sherman Avenue, and following it to the intersection with Short Sherman Avenue.

Alternatively, drive north on Halls Ferry Road to Clay Street. Turn left on Clay, then right on U.S. 61 BUS and take it past Vicksburg National Cemetery (you will see Vicksburg National Cemetery Memorial Arch). Turn right on Sherman Avenue, and follow that to the intersection with Short Sherman Avenue.

Appendix A
Glossary of Terms for Memorial Art and Architecture

Alto relief: High relief. See Bas-relief.

Bas-relief (pronounced bah, a French term): Low relief. A sculpture in relief (rather than in the round, or fully formed in three dimensions) is primarily a two-dimensional sculpture that has its background elements relieved from its primary forms in the foreground planes. All of the portrait reliefs of brigade and commanders mounted on free-standing stone stelae at Vicksburg are relatively low relief. Few, if any, forms are undercut. In contrast, the six pictorial narrative panels on the *Iowa Monument* are "alto," or high relief. Some of the figures in those panels are nearly free from the background above their waists.

Beaux Arts (pronounced boze are, another French term): An adjective referring to art or architecture (also artists and architects) associated with the state-funded École des Beaux-Arts (school of beautiful arts) in Paris. Only the best students and teachers worked at the École, where art and architecture were taught in rigorous classes rooted in drawing from nature and learning from revered examples of classical art and architecture. The Beaux Arts style popular in the United States from the World's Columbian Exposition in Chicago in 1893 until the Great Depression of the 1930s features invigorated modeling of sculptural forms and the integration of sculpture and architecture, as seen in the Missouri and Iowa monuments.

Bronze: A copper-rich alloy usually containing lead, tin, and zinc, and other trace elements. Traditional "monumental" bronze is "85 three five," or 85% copper and 5% each of lead, tin, and zinc, although metallurgical tests of early-twentieth-century bronzes show minor variations. Silicon bronze (copper plus 2–3% silicon) has become the industry standard in recent years because of its ductility and the absence of lead, a health hazard. Bronze casts are hollow shells approximately $\frac{1}{4}$ to $\frac{3}{8}$ inches thick.

Bust: A bust-length portrait of a person. Those at Vicksburg typically include the shoulders and extend to the middle of the chest. The head is usually modeled in three dimensions, but the back of the body is often simplified or reduced to a smooth, unarticulated surface.

Casting: The process of casting bronze in molds made from models. For more information on the process, see the text sections on bronze casting.

City Beautiful Movement: An effort to improve the appearance of urban areas between the 1893 World's Columbian Exposition in Chicago and the U.S. entry into World War I. The temporary "White City" of the Columbian Exposition featured Classical Revival architecture, most of which was made of wood and covered with white plaster ornament, including abundant figurative sculpture made in staff, a mixture of plaster of Paris and hemp or straw. The "White City" stimulated the popularity of the Classical Revival style, especially for public buildings, during an era when civic reformers razed slums and built new public buildings like the libraries in New York City and Boston.

Content: Meaning.

Exedra (plural exedrae): A seat or bench; in particular, a monument, pedestal, or base (like those of the Missouri and Pennsylvania monuments) that includes a long, low seat or bench that may curve forward. Exedrae were common monument forms during the City Beautiful Movement when the Classical Revival style popularized these ancient Roman forms. See figs. 11.1, DT42.

Form: Shape. Sculptors give ideas form by shaping clay, stone, bronze, or other media into geometric or biomorphic forms. The spaces between positive forms are negative forms.

Modeling: The process of building up sculptural forms by adding modeling clay and working it with rakes and other tools to texture the surface.

Molds: Negative forms used to cast positive sculptural forms. Plaster piece molds are poured around wax or clay original sculptures and used to make plaster positives or models that can have sand packed around them to make green sand or French sand molds to cast bronze.

Obelisk: A tall, thin, tapering shaft that is square in plan and topped with a pyramid. Obelisks were used in ancient Egypt and thus became associated with funerary art and architecture. They were popular in ancient Rome, in the Renaissance, and in the nineteenth and twentieth centuries in the United States.

Patina (pa tin´ a, or pat´ in a): The coloration of bronze. Patination is a chemical process that occurs in the foundry with the application of ferrous and sulfuric compounds to the raw cast bronze to change its color from the bright copper of a new penny to darker and richer tones of green, brown, and black. Patination also occurs naturally once bronze is placed in an outdoor environment where water and airborne chemicals change its color and texture, often streaking and camouflaging the sculptural forms in ways not intended by the artists.

Pointing machine: An apparatus that translates points from one model to another. Pointing machines are used by carvers to measure their stone carvings against the original model, which is usually in plaster. Pointing machines can also be used to enlarge a quarter-scale or one-third scale model to a full-scale model by adjusting the fittings on the machine. In fact, pointing machines merely indicate the points in space that correspond to points on the model. The sculptor must build up the model or carve down the stone to match the points.

Relief: A sculpture in relief (rather than in the round, or fully formed in three dimensions) is a primarily two-dimensional sculpture that has its background plane relieved from its primary forms in the raised foreground. See Alto Relief and Bas-relief.

Stele (pronounced steel´ ee, plural stelae): A stone slab or form that is taller than it is broad or deep. Stelae support portrait reliefs at Vicksburg. They are also incorporated into exedrae like those of the Pennsylvania and Missouri monuments.

Appendix B
Biographical Sketches of Artists, Architects, Foundries, and Monument Companies with Memorial Art at Vicksburg National Military Park

Additional information about most of these people and companies can be found in the Smithsonian's online Inventory of American Sculpture (IAS), but that resource is listed as a reference for individual biographical sketches only if it is a major source for information about the subject. The IAS provides descriptive and location information on sculpture by American artists in public and private collections worldwide.

Adams, Herbert (1858–1945), *Michigan Monument*

Adams studied art in Boston before traveling to Paris, where he studied with Antonin Mercié at the École des Beaux-Arts from 1885 to 1890 and won an honorable mention at an exhibition in 1888–89. He created several distinctive polychromed and multimedia portrait and ideal busts of women about that time, which earned him renown for their delicate and decorative qualities. These busts and his reliefs are influenced by his study of spontaneous French modeling techniques, the work of Augustus Saint-Gaudens, and Florentine Renaissance art. He was a master of bas-relief and executed bronze doors for several buildings as well as statuary for exterior and interior architectural settings. His best-known monumental sculptures are his *William Ellery Channing,* in Boston's Public Garden (1903), and *William Cullen Bryant,* behind the New York Public Library (1911). Both are set against Renaissance revival exedrae and designed in conjunction with architects. He also created a portrait figure of Gen. Andrew Humphries for the National Cemetery in Fredericksburg, Virginia, and numerous other monumental portraits. Adams exhibited at the World's Columbian Exposition, Chicago (1893); the Pan-American Exposition, Buffalo (1901); the Louisiana Purchase Exposition, St. Louis (1904); and the Panama-Pacific Exposition, San Francisco (1915).

Adams was a founder of the National Sculpture Society in 1893 and served as its president twice, from 1908 to 1910 and from 1912 to 1914. He was also its honorary president from 1933 until his death. He was an academician of the National Academy of Design and was its president from 1917 to 1920—one of only three sculptors to hold that position. Adams was a modest, sensitive, and retiring person who was respected for his fine nature and firm sense of fairness.

References: Adams 1929; Bach 1992; Caffin 1913; Gayle and Cohen 1988; Gurney 1985; National Sculpture Society 1929; Panhorst 1999; Proske 1943; Proske 1955; Reynolds 1988; Small 1982.

American Bronze Company, American Bronze Foundry Company, American Art Bronze, all of Chicago, Illinois, *Missouri Monument* bronzes, 3 busts, 2 figures

The American Bronze Company was active in Chicago by ca. 1888, and the American Bronze Foundry Company was formed by ca. 1898. Jules Berchem was superintendent of both companies by about 1898. American Art Bronze Foundry appears to be a foundry mark used between 1917 and 1919. Berchem was also the principal of the Florentine Brotherhood Foundry, which was active in Chicago around 1918, and the sculptor of at least one monumental bronze figure, the *Robert Buckner Monument,* Dallas, Texas (dedicated 1936, with American Bronze Company foundry mark).

Major castings include the equestrian *General Grant Monument* by Robert Bringhurst for St. Louis (1888); statues of Salmon Chase and Edwin Stanton for Levi Schofield's *These Are My Jewels Monument* on the state capitol grounds in Columbus, Ohio (1891); and Lorado Taft, *Eternal Silence,* Chicago (1909).

References: Bach and Gray 1983; Gurney 1985; Roman Bronze Works Archives; Shapiro 1985.

A.R.T. Research Enterprises, Lancaster, Pennsylvania, Lincoln and Davis bronze figure castings for *Kentucky Monument*

The company is a full-service fine arts foundry established in 1978. It uses traditional as well as innovative technology and methodology, utilizing ceramic shell mold-making for lost wax casts while also working with sand molds. It casts bronze, aluminum, and stainless steel; paints and patinates what it makes; and offers sculpture restoration services, model enlargements, and rapid prototyping.

Major castings include *West Virginia Veterans Memorial,* Charleston, West Virginia (1995–1999); Wendy Ross, *George Mason National Memorial,* Washington, D.C. (2002); Gary Casteel, *U.S. Colored Troops Monument,* Lexington Park, Maryland (2012).

Reference: www.thinksculpture.com.

Berchem, Jules (1855–1930), *Missouri Monument* bronze castings, Grant equestrian, 2 figures, 2 busts, 11 reliefs

Berchem was a founder and an entrepreneur who operated American Bronze Company, American Bronze Foundry Company, American Art Bronze Company, and the Florentine Brotherhood Foundry, all in Chicago. Berchem was born in Paris and began foundry work as a child. He moved to Chicago in 1885 and is buried in St. Joseph Cemetery, River Grove, Illinois. See American Bronze Company for additional information.

Reference: Bach and Gray 1983.

Borglum, Solon H. (1868–1922), 5 busts, 1 relief

Solon Hannibal Borglum was the younger brother of Gutzon Borglum, the sculptor of Mt. Rushmore. Solon grew up in Nebraska, where he gained an abiding interest in nature, wild animals, and Native Americans, which manifested itself in popular figure groups of cowboys and Indians similar to those by Frederic Remington. He studied art in Cincinnati and Paris and opened a studio in New York in 1900. He exhibited at the Buffalo (1901), St. Louis (1904), and San Francisco (1915) expositions and was elected to the National Sculpture Society in 1902. His thorough knowledge of horses contributed to the success of his equestrian monuments to Gen. John Gordon, Atlanta (1907) and Rough Rider Bucky O'Neill, Prescott, Arizona (1907).

References: Adams 1929; Craven 1984; Gayle and Cohen 1988; Gurney 1985; Proske 1943; Proske 1955; Reynolds 1988.

Brewster, George T. (1862–1943), 2 statues, 8 busts, 18 reliefs

Brewster taught at the Art Students League and Cooper Union. He made two figures for the Brooklyn Museum; an equestrian sculpture of W. P. Hussy for Danvers, Massachusetts; soldiers monuments for Malden, Massachusetts, and Athens, Pennsylvania; and *Indiana,* to crown the colossal *Indiana Soldiers and Sailors Monument* in Indianapolis. He also made the *Fountain of Nature* for the Buffalo exposition (1901).

Reference: Taft 1924.

Bureau Brothers, Philadelphia, Pennsylvania

Achille Bureau emigrated from France to Philadelphia ca. 1860, and his brother Edouard arrived in 1869. They worked for Robert Wood and Company until it closed in the late 1870s and then formed Bureau Brothers and Heaton in 1879. Sons Edmund and Edouard took over management in the 1880s. They operated as Bureau Brothers from 1883 until the company closed ca. 1940.

Major castings include Augustus Saint-Gaudens, *Adams Memorial,* Washington, D.C. (1890); Daniel Chester French and Edward Potter's equestrian *General Grant Monument,* Philadelphia (1897); H. K. Bush-Brown's equestrian *General Sedgwick Monument,* Gettysburg (1913).

References: Bach 1992; Shapiro 1985.

Casteel, Gary (born 1946), 2 statues on *Kentucky Monument*

Casteel was born in West Virginia. He studied sculpture in Florence and Pietrasanta, Italy, and apprenticed with sculptors Russell Rote in New York and Salvatore Lopez in Miami. He has specialized in sculpture with Civil War subjects, including the creation of small versions of battlefield monuments marketed to raise funds for restoration of the memorials. His 54th Volunteer Infantry Monument, Johnstown, Pennsylvania (2000), replaces one destroyed in a flood.

He created the equestrian *Gen. James Longstreet Monument,* Gettysburg (1998); *Confederate Prisoner of War Memorial,* Point Lookout, Maryland (2008); *13th North Carolina Monument,* South Mountain Battlefield, Hagerstown, Maryland; *Brothers Memorial,* Spotsylvania Court House, Virginia; and *U.S. Colored Troops Monument,* Lexington Park, Maryland.

His work is in the collections of Gettysburg College, Virginia Military Institute, Museum of the Confederacy, Carlisle War College, and the national military parks at Fredericksburg and Ft. Donelson. He has also created numerous relief portraits and the Civil War Institute Medallion.

References: Inventory of American Sculpture; www.garycasteel.com.

Cianfarani, Aristide Berto (1895–1960), 1 bust

Cianfarani worked with Gorham Company Founders and produced several monumental sculptures and memorials, most of which were located around New England: *Bandmaster Bowen Church Monument,* Providence, Rhode Island (1928); *Fox Point Veterans Memorial,* Providence, Rhode Island (1946); *Prince Henry the Navigator Monument,* Fall River, Massachusetts (1940); *Gen. Peter Muhlenberg Monument,* Muhlenberg College, Allentown, Pennsylvania (1941); *Lieutenant Power Memorial,* Worcester, Massachusetts (1947); *World War I Memorial,* Meriden, Connecticut (1930); *The Victor, Box Elder County World War I and II Memorial,* Brigham City, Utah.

References: Inventory of American Sculpture; Gurney 1985; Reynolds 1988.

Coe, Herring (1907–1999), figure on *Texas Monument*

Coe trained as an engineer before studying sculpture with Carl Milles at Cranbrook Academy of Art in Bloomfield Hills, Michigan. In the 1930s he carved 37 limestone reliefs as part of a public works project for the city hall in Houston, Texas. He also provided architectural sculpture for Houston's St. Mary's Seminary Chapel, St. Placidus Home for the Aged, First Presbyterian Church, and the library of Rice University, as well as entry pylons (1952) for the Hermann Park Zoo and ornamentation for its Reptile Building. Coe also created bas-reliefs for the Biology–Geology Building at Lamar State College in Beaumont and a granite frieze for the *New London School Memorial.* His bronze statue of Confederate Lieutenant Dick Dowling at Sabine Pass was funded by the Texas Centennial Commission in 1936. Coe also created medallic art, producing the 75th issue of the Society of Medalists in 1967 and exhibiting at the biennial congress of Federation Internationale de la Medaille in Lisbon in 1979. He served in the Seabees in World War II, then practiced in Beaumont for the rest of his life.

References: Little 1996; Salmon 1993; Society of Medalists 1967.

Cottrell, W. Liance (1868–1964), *Wisconsin Monument*

Cottrell was an architect of fashionable homes and expensive mausoleums (most in New England) as well as two of the largest Civil War battlefield monuments built in the early twentieth century—the *Pennsylvania Monument* at Gettysburg (1910) and the *Wisconsin Monument* at Vicksburg. Cottrell was born in Westerly, Rhode Island. He studied architecture at the Metropolitan Museum of Art and attended lectures under William R. Ware at Columbia University. He also attended the Art Students League and took classes in modeling under J. Q. A. Ward. Throughout his career he was associated with Harrison Granite Company, New York, a major producer and trader in stone and monuments. Cottrell kept an office in New York (probably with Harrison), but lived and worked at The Boulders, the home he built in Stonington, Connecticut. He was retired during the final forty years of his life.

Reference: Panhorst 1988.

Couper, William (1853–1942), *Minnesota Monument*, 2 statues, 3 busts

Couper was born in Norfolk, Virginia, and was introduced to sculpture and monuments through his father's firm, Couper Marble Works, in Richmond, Virginia. He studied at Cooper Institute, New York, and then trained at the Academy of Fine Arts and the Royal College of Surgery in Munich in 1874. In 1875 he traveled to Florence, where Thomas Ball invited him to work in his studio. Over the course of two decades, Couper absorbed the essence of Ball's neoclassical style. He married Ball's daughter in 1878. Couper returned to the United States with Ball in 1897 and they shared a studio in New York.

Couper produced an abundance of public and private works, including funerary monuments and architectural sculpture. He finished Ball's seated figure of Longfellow for Washington, D.C. (1909), and made the figure of Moses for the Appellate Court in New York City. He produced a portrait of President McKinley for Scranton, Pennsylvania; a memorial to Revolutionary War sailors for Annapolis, Maryland; and an ideal figure called *Beauty's Wreath for Valor's Brow.*

Lorado Taft admired his many angels, whose eternally youthful faces and sensitively modeled features imbue the sculptures with the calm and quiet gracefulness that is at the root of neoclassical art. Taft also recognized the "large monumental qualities . . . simplicity and repose" in his work (Taft 1924, 424).

References: Couper 1988; Hendry 1980; Gayle and Cohen 1988; Taft 1924.

Crunelle, Leonard (1872–1944), *General Logan*

Crunelle was born in Lens, France, and immigrated as a child to Decatur, Illinois. The young Crunelle followed his father to work as a miner, and he began to model figures in clay. Lorado Taft discovered the young man's talent during one of his many lecture tours in the Midwest. Taft asked Crunelle to assist with the sculptural decoration of the temporary Beaux Arts buildings of the World's Columbian Exposition in Chicago in 1893; Crunelle then became Taft's principal assistant until his mentor's death in 1936.

Crunelle created many monuments, fountains, and architectural decorations in the Midwest, including the *Richard Oglesby Monument* (1919); the *Black Soldiers Monument* (ded. 1927, finial figure added 1936); *Squirrel Boy* and additional garden sculptures in public parks, all in Chicago; *Lincoln Monument,* Freeport, Illinois (1929); and *Hixon Memorial,* La Crosse, Wisconsin.

References: Bach and Gray 1983; McDougal 1908; Riedy 1981; Taft 1924.

Elwell, Francis Edwin (1858–1922), *Rhode Island Monument,* 2 statues, 1 bust, 2 reliefs

Elwell grew up in Concord, Massachusetts, and (like Daniel Chester French) had his first art lessons with Abigail May Alcott. He travelled to Paris in 1878 and studied with Alexandre Falguière and François Jouffroy at the École des Beaux-Arts, exhibiting a monumental figure at the Salon of 1885. By 1885, he was in New York, sharing a studio with French and teaching at the Art Students League and the National Academy of Design. He participated in the expositions in Chicago (1893) and Buffalo (1901), and made statuary for the New York Customs House, as well as portraits for the U.S. Capitol, and the equestrian statue of General Hancock, Gettysburg (1896). Taft was enamored with the style and content of his sculpture, noting that his "execution varies much with his moods . . . he always has something to say, and says it in a manner so original, so different from the expression of others, that he is almost invariably interesting" (Taft 1924, 412). Elwell served briefly as curator of sculpture for the Metropolitan Museum of Art, but his personality often left him at odds with others. He gradually withdrew from sculpture during the last decade of his life.

References: Adams 1929; Taft 1924.

Florentine Brotherhood Foundry, Chicago, *Grant* equestrian casting

See American Bronze Company and Jules Berchem.

Ganiere, George Etienne (1865–1935), 2 busts, 6 reliefs

Ganiere's career was centered around Chicago. His bronzes for Vicksburg were cast there by Jules Berchem's various foundry ventures, as were his equestrian *Anthony Wayne Monument,* Ft. Wayne, Indiana (1918), and his statues of Abraham Lincoln for monuments in Burlington, Wisconsin (1913, in association with Lorado Taft) and Webster City, Iowa (1913). Plaster models for his Lincoln (1916) and Stephen Douglas (1916) are at the Chicago Historical Society and a plaster Lincoln (1916) is at the Milwaukee Art Museum.

Reference: Inventory of American Sculpture.

Gorham Company Founders, Providence, Rhode Island, *Tilghman* equestrian casting and 79 other figures, busts, and reliefs

Gorham is best known for silver, which it has designed and fabricated since 1824. From the early 1880s through the 1950s Gorham also operated a bronze foundry, initially as an outgrowth of its burgeoning business in ecclesiastical objects such as lecterns and decorative castings. Over the years, Gorham's quality has been consistently among the best in the business. It has cast many important monumental and small-scale sculptures as well as decorative objects and architectural ornamentation.

Gorham's first monumental bronze was Frederick Kohlhagen's *Skirmisher* on the *Tenth Pennsylvania Reserve Infantry [39th Regiment] Monument* at Gettysburg (1889). In 1896 Gorham made the first lost-wax casting in the United States, and between 1901 and 1906 it built an addition to its New York foundry specifically for working in lost wax. France's best lost-wax founder, Pierre Bingen, joined Gorham in 1906.

Major castings include Augustus Saint-Gaudens, *Robert Gould Shaw Memorial,* Boston (1897); Gutzon Borglum's equestrian *General Sheridan Monument,* Washington, D.C.; Daniel Chester French, *Spencer Trask Fountain,* Saratoga Springs, New York (1915). Gorham also cast all except the first of Theo Kitson's 52 *Hikers.*

References: Ames and Panhorst 1985; Carpenter 1982, Shapiro 1985.

G. Vignali Foundry, Florence, Italy, Mississippi Monument Castings

The company was active from the nineteenth century through most of the twentieth. Frederick Ernst Triebel and George Bissell (1839–1920) appear to have been the only notable Americans to use monumental Vignali bronze castings in the United States during the early twentieth century. Several prominent American artists, such as Paul Manship (1885–1966), Charles Umlauf (1911–1994), Harry Jackson (1924–2011), Stanley Bleifeld (born 1924), and Bruno Lucchesi (born 1926), used Vignali and Tommasi Fonderia d'Arte during the middle and late twentieth century when its facilities were located at Pietrasanta, a popular arts center and quaint quarry village near Florence that had supplied Michelangelo and other Renaissance artists with their raw material. Vignali also operated a subsidiary in Pretoria, South Africa, from 1931 until about 1960.

References: Inventory of American Sculpture; Panhorst 1988.

Hibbard, Frederick C. (1881–1950), *General Grant* equestrian statue, eagle on *Illinois Memorial,* 1 bust

Hibbard moved from Canton, Missouri, to study with Lorado Taft at the Art Institute of Chicago and then settled in Chicago's Hyde Park. He and his wife, Elizabeth Haseltine Hibbard, were both sculptors; they collaborated on the *David Wallach Fountain* in Chicago. Frederick also made two large eagles (1931) for Hyde Park; the *Greene Vardiman Black Monument* (1918) for Lincoln Park; the *Carter Henry Harrison Monument* (1907) for Union Park; and many more public and private sculptures. His elaborate exedral monument to the Confederacy, known as the *United Daughters of the Confederacy Memorial* because of their patronage of the structure, was dedicated at Shiloh National Military Park in Tennessee in 1917. Several of Hibbard's working models are preserved at the Chicago Historical Society.

References: Bach and Gray 1893; McDougal 1908; Panhorst, 1988; Riedy 1981.

Holm, Victor S. (1876–1935), *Missouri Monument,* 6 reliefs

Holm was born in Copenhagen, immigrated to the United States in 1889, and studied with Lorado Taft at the Art Institute of Chicago. He also studied at the Art Students League in New York and worked in the studio of Philip Martiny, a prominent sculptor responsible for many fine architectural decorations. He became instructor of sculpture at Washington University in St. Louis in 1909.

Holm won medals at the Missouri State Fair in 1913 and the St. Louis Artists' Guild in 1914, 1916, and 1917; an honorable mention in the San Francisco exposition (1915); as well as other honors during his long and productive career. He was a member of the National Sculpture Society and the St. Louis Artists' Guild, Art League, and Architectural Club.

Holm's oeuvre includes the *Luman Parker Monument,* Rolla, Missouri; the *Thomas Carlin Monument,* Carrollton, Illinois; the *Washington Fischel Monument,* St. Louis; the *Colonel Drieux Monument,* New Orleans, Louisiana; and a World War I Memorial for Maplewood, Missouri. He also made numerous fountains, funerary memorials, and architectural decorations located in Missouri, Illinois, and Iowa.

Reference: National Sculpture Society 1929.

Hughes Granite Company; Clyde, Ohio; 39 Ohio unit memorials

Formed in the 1880s, the company designed and built monuments, markers, and mausoleums. Like most monument companies at the turn of the century, it used steam engines to run saws, planers, and lifting machinery, and pneumatic power for carving and lettering. William E. Hughes managed the company until his death in 1921. Hughes also operated the American Mausoleum Company and the American Mausoleum Construction Company, which were responsible collectively for more than a hundred mausoleums nationwide. Hughes employed as many as 55 employees, including James B. King, a sculptor who eventually became a partner in the company. Its most notable monument is a colossal column and allegorical figure all in granite at Antietam National Battlefield, where future president and native Ohioan William McKinley achieved fame for his martial exploits.

Reference: www.sandusky-county-scrapbook.net/Hughes.htm.

Jenny, William Le Baron (1832–1907), *Illinois Memorial*

Jenny was born to an affluent whaling ship owner in Fairhaven, Massachusetts. He attended Philips Academy in Andover, Massachusetts, and the Lawrence Scientific School at Harvard, then studied architecture and engineering at the École des Arts et Manufactures in Paris, graduating in 1856. He worked with a railroad in Mexico until the outbreak of the Civil War, when he joined the U.S. Army Corps of Engineers, serving under generals Sherman and Grant, and rising to the rank of major. After the war he opened an office in Chicago, specializing in commercial buildings and civil engineering. Many young architects of the Chicago School apprenticed with him. He designed the ten-story Home Insurance Office Building in Chicago (1884–1885), the first fireproof, metal-framed skyscraper, and other tall buildings with innovative structural features, which earned him the moniker "Father of the Skyscraper." He also designed the Horticulture Building for the Columbian Exposition (1893). He was a Fellow of the American Institute of Architects.

Reference: Turak 1986.

John Williams Foundry and John Williams, Inc., 2 figures, 6 busts, 6 reliefs

Williams worked for Tiffany & Co. as a designer before going into business for himself in New York in 1875. John Williams Foundry was incorporated in 1905 and dissolved in 1953. The namesake of the foundry died in 1914. Major castings include Olin Levi Warner's doors for the Library of Congress in Washington, D.C. (1892) and Daniel Chester French's doors for the Boston Public Library (1903).

Reference: Shapiro 1985.

Kitson, Henry Hudson (1863–1947), *Iowa Monument,* 3 statues, 4 busts, 2 reliefs

Kitson was born in Huddersfield, Yorkshire, England, and immigrated to the United States to work with his older brothers John William and Samuel in New York. He worked on the William B. Astor Memorial (1877) in Trinity Church and on William Vanderbilt's Fifth Avenue mansion (1883). His *Music of the Sea* (cast in bronze in 1884), now in the Museum of Fine Arts, Boston, was a salon success. Kitson opened a studio in Boston in 1886. His first student and protégé, Theo Alice Ruggles, became his wife in 1893. His 1888 portrait of her has been recognized as "an affecting portrait of uncommon power" that "seems almost breathing and warm with life" (Greenthal et al. 1986, 305).

The Kitsons collaborated on numerous sculptural projects, including the *Minuteman,* Waltham, Massachusetts (1905); *Patrick Andrew Collins Monument,* Boston (1908); and *Richard Saltonstall Monument,* Watertown, Massachusetts (1931). They separated around 1909 but never divorced.

Other major works of his include the *Admiral Farragut Monument,* Boston (1893); *Minuteman Monument,* Lexington, (1900); *Nathaniel Banks Monument,* Waltham (1908); *Roger Conant Monument,* Salem (1913); *Robert Burns Monument,* Boston (1917); *Pilgrim Maiden,* Plymouth (1924); and the heroic-scale bronze portrait figure of *Gen. Lloyd Tilghman,* Paducah, Kentucky (1909).

References: Greenthal et al. 1986; Kitson Papers, New York Historical Society; Henry and Theo Alice Ruggles Kitson Papers, Archives of American Art, Smithsonian Institution.

Kitson, Theodora Alice Ruggles (1871–1932), *Massachusetts Monument,* assisted with *Iowa Monument,* 19 busts, 52 reliefs

Ruggles was a child prodigy born into a wealthy Boston family. Unable to obtain art training at the School of the Museum of Fine Arts because of her gender, she studied in Henry Kitson's private studio in 1886 and 1887. In 1887 she and her mother went to Paris, where she studied with Pascal Dagnan-Bouveret and Gustave Courtois. She exhibited in the salons of 1888, 1889, and 1890, and at the Exposition Universelle (1890), winning honorable mentions at the salons of 1888 and 1889 and the Exposition Universelle—a remarkable achievement for any young artist and unprecedented for a female sculptor. Upon her return to the United States, she showed sculpture at the Columbian (1893) and St. Louis (1904) expositions, winning a bronze medal for her *Volunteer* for Newburyport, Massachusetts (1902).

In 1893 she married Henry Kitson. They had three children before separating around 1909; they never divorced. Theo assisted Henry with the *Minuteman,* Waltham, Massachusetts (1905); the *Patrick Andrew Collins Monument,* Boston (1908); and the *Richard Saltonstall Monument,* Watertown, Massachusetts (1931); as well as the *Iowa Monument* at Vicksburg.

In 1902 her *Volunteer* was dedicated in Newburyport, Massachusetts, and the State of Massachusetts commissioned a slightly revised replica for Vicksburg. The Newburyport *Volunteer* has a pine bough on the plinth between the feet of the figure and no bedroll over the shoulder. The *Volunteer* was subsequently replicated as a Civil War monument in North Providence, Rhode Island (1904); Ashburnham, Massachusetts (1904); Walden, New York (1905); Pasadena, California (1906); Sharon, Massachusetts (1906–7); Westbrook, Maine (1917); and Townsend, Massachusetts (1932).

Multiple copies of monumental bronzes are not common, but Theo's *Hiker,* the stolid figure of a Spanish-American War soldier first commissioned by the University of Minnesota in 1906 was subsequently replicated for placement in 51 other locations nationwide. All except the first of these casts were made by Gorham.

She also made the *Mother Bickerdyke Monument,* Galesburg, Illinois (1906) and the *Tadeusz Kosciuszko Monument,* Boston (1927).

References: Ames and Panhorst 1985; Greenthal et al. 1986; Kitson Papers, New York Historical Society; Henry and Theo Kitson Papers, Archives of American Art; Rubenstein 1990.

Lawhon, Charles L. (1872–1926), *National Memorial and Peace Jubilee Memorial Arch*

Lawhon designed memorial art and architecture, serving as the chief designer for the Albert Weiblen Marble and Granite Company in New Orleans for many years. He was associated with the Tennessee Marble Works for the last few years of his life and died in Knoxville.

Reference: Albert Weiblen Marble and Granite Company Records.

Loester, Julius C. (ca. 1860–1923), statuary for *Wisconsin Monument*

Loester studied abroad and taught wood and marble carving in Munich and Vienna. He also taught sculpture and ornamental modeling at the Mechanics Institute in New York. He executed many memorials, especially for New York and New Jersey locations, in the 45 years he lived in America and is best known for his *Doughboy* memorials. Loester's major works include a heroic-scale bronze copy of *Whistler's Mother,* which he made with Emil Siebern for Ashland, Pennsylvania (1938).

References: Inventory of American Sculpture; Panhorst 1988.

Lopez, Charles Albert (1869–1906), 5 reliefs on *Pennsylvania Monument*

Lopez was born in Mexico and moved to New York as a young man. He studied with J. Q. A. Ward and at the École des Beaux-Arts in Paris. He contributed to the temporary *Dewey Memorial Arch* in New York (1899) and was commissioned to make a monument to William McKinley for Philadelphia. He finished the working models for the portrait figure and an allegorical group of *Wisdom Instructing Youth* but then died unexpectedly. Isidore Konti (1862–1938) completed the monument.

Reference: Bach 1992.

Lowell, Guy (1870–1927), architectural services for Henry Kitson's *Iowa Monument*

Born into Boston's prominent Lowell family, Guy attended private school, graduated from Harvard College (1892) and the Massachusetts Institute of Technology (1894), and studied landscape horticulture at the Royal Botanic Gardens, Kew, England, and architectural history at the École des Beaux-Arts, Paris. In 1899 he opened an office in Boston and by 1906 another in New York City. His commissions included palatial homes and gardens as well as public and commercial buildings. He designed five structures for Boston's Charles River Dam (1910) and extended Frederick Law Olmsted's Charlesbank into the Boston Embankment now known as the Esplanade. Lowell designed the Museum of Fine Arts, Boston (1906–9); New York State Supreme Court Building, New York City (1912–14 and 1919–27); and buildings at Philips Academy, Andover, Massachusetts; as well as gardens for J. P. Morgan and Andrew Carnegie. He led an influential landscape architecture program at M.I.T. (1900–1910) that trained many important designers, including women, who had few other educational opportunities in that field. Lowell also published several significant books and periodical essays.

Reference: Birnbaum and Karson 2000.

McKenzie, R. Tait (1867–1938), 2 busts flanking walk to *Pennsylvania Monument*

McKenzie was accomplished in art, medicine, and physical education. He studied medicine at McGill University and practiced as a physician and lecturer on anatomy before becoming professor of physical education at the University of Pennsylvania in 1904. His earliest sculptures were models of athletes for clinical study. He designed many medals for athletic contests, some of which are still in use today. In his life as in his art, McKenzie embraced the classical ideal of the well-rounded man— "the eager mind in a lithe body" (Kozar 1975, vii).

During the first decade of the twentieth century he exhibited at the Salon in Paris and the Royal Academy of Art in London. McKenzie won medals at the St. Louis (1904) and San Francisco (1915) expositions and the king's medal (1912) in Sweden. He was a member of the Philadelphia Art Club and the Fellowship of the Pennsylvania Academy of Fine Arts.

His *Boy Scout Memorial* was commissioned by the scouts in 1937 for Pittsburgh and was replicated for many years for placement in at least two dozen cities. He made an energetic *Youthful Benjamin Franklin* and a portrait of George Whitfield for Philadelphia; the *Volunteer Monument,* Almonte, Canada; the *Homecoming Victory Memorial,* Cambridge, England; and the *Scottish-American Memorial,* Edinburgh, Scotland. Other works are in Stockholm, Sweden, and Oxford, England.

References: Evert 1983; Kozar 1975; National Sculpture Society 1929; Proske 1943.

Milione, Louis (1884–1955), 1 bust, 1 relief

Little is known about Milione, who made the west pediment of Philadelphia's Municipal Courthouse (ca. 1935) and state shields for its Federal Courthouse and Post Office (1934–1940).

Reference: Bach 1992.

Modern Art Foundry, New York, cast *Alabama Monument* and *General Forney* figure

The company, founded by John Spring in 1932, is now operated by two of his grandchildren in Astoria, New York. In its eight decades of operation it has produced more than 15,000 sculptures for some of the most important artists of the day. The company uses traditional as well as innovative techniques and offers a wide range of foundry services, including enlarging, molding, casting, finishing, patination, and installation as well as maintenance and conservation.

References: http://www.modernartfoundry.com/about.html; Inventory of American Sculpture.

Muldoon Monument Company, Louisville, Kentucky, *Kentucky Monument*

Muldoon was one of the largest and best-known monument companies in the country at the turn of the twentieth century. It was also one of the most completely diversified. As early as 1871, Mike Muldoon employed over 300 in his Louisville plant. In the early 1870s Muldoon also had marble yards in St. Louis, Memphis, and New Orleans. The company quarried stone for general construction as well as monumental work. It also built buildings and monuments, but Muldoon specialized in cutting and setting elaborately decorated tombstones and public monuments. It was a major supplier of funerary monuments, mausoleums, and civic and battlefield memorials throughout the lower Midwest and the South during the late nineteenth and early twentieth centuries. The company's location on the south side of the Ohio River gave it a competitive advantage with Southern patrons of Civil War monuments even though most of the sculptors and foundries Muldoon contracted for statuary on its Confederate memorials were active in the North. That location surely influenced the patrons of the *Kentucky Monument* at the end of the twentieth century when they selected their native sons to design and build the memorial to their Civil War ancestors.

Reference: Panhorst 1988.

Mulligan, Charles J. (1866–1916), 3 busts on *Illinois Memorial*

Mulligan was an Irish immigrant marble carver. Lorado Taft discovered him and made him foreman of his mammoth studio, which fabricated sculpture for Chicago's Columbian Exposition (1893). Taft recognized that Mulligan's "strong right hand has within its grasp the delicacy and precision which come from long and patient training" (Taft 1924, 527). Mulligan later succeeded Taft at the Art Institute of Chicago.

His *Digger* was intended to commemorate the construction of the drainage canal in Chicago. It was shown at the Buffalo exposition (1901) but was never completed as a permanent memorial. Other works include *Lincoln the Railsplitter,* Chicago (1911), replicated for Burlington,

Wisconsin (ca. 1913); *Lincoln at Gettysburg,* Pana, Illinois, replicated for Chicago (ca. 1905); a marble *Miner and His Child,* Chicago (1911); *William McKinley,* Chicago (1905); and *Independence Fountain,* Chicago (1902).

References: Bach and Gray 1983; Riedy 1981.

Newman, Allen G. (1875–1940), 2 reliefs

Newman was born in New York City and studied with J. Q. A. Ward from 1897 to 1901. He also studied at the National Academy of Design. He was a member of the National Sculpture Society, American Federation of Arts, American Numismatic Society, Beaux-Arts Institute of Design; an associate of the National Academy of Design; and he belonged to the National Arts Club, which awarded him a prize.

He made two monumental figures that were replicated for Spanish-American and World War I memorials. Lorado Taft claimed that his *Hiker* "has been pronounced by more than one critic 'the best bronze soldier in America'" (Taft 1924, 570). His *Hikers* are in Ann Arbor, Michigan and in Buffalo and Staten Island, New York. A *Doughboy* is in Pittsburgh, Pennsylvania. He was also responsible for the *Triumph of Peace Monument,* Atlanta, Georgia; *Women of the South Monument,* Jacksonville, Florida; and the *Pioneer Monument,* Salem, Oregon. He made portrait memorials to Gen. Philip Sheridan, Scranton, Pennsylvania; Gov. William Oates, Montgomery, Alabama; and Lord Harris, Caracas, Venezuela.

References: Evert 1983; Keller and Curtis 1995; National Sculpture Society 1929; Taft 1924.

Perry, Roland Hinton (1870–1941), 6 busts, 2 reliefs

Perry was born in New York. He studied at the Art Students League and in Paris from 1890 to 1894 at the École des Beaux-Arts, Academie Julian, and Academie Delacleuse. Upon opening a studio in New York, he was commissioned to make the *Neptune Fountain* for the Library of Congress in Washington, D.C. He also made the large bronze figures of a Union and Confederate soldier shaking hands atop the colossal *New York State Peace Monument* on Lookout Mountain, Chickamauga–Chattanooga National Military Park (1910). Other major works include portrait figures of generals Greene (1907) and Wadsworth (1914) at Gettysburg; Langdon Doors, Buffalo Historical Society (1901); an equestrian statue of General Castleman, Louisville, Kentucky; and Dr. Benjamin Rush and the lions on Taft Bridge, both in Washington, D.C. He also executed the colossal bronze female figure designed by James Huston, architect of the Pennsylvania State Capitol, for the top of that building's dome.

References: Panhorst 1988; Small 1982.

Potter, Edward Clark (1857–1923), *General McClernand* equestrian statue

Potter apprenticed in the studio of Daniel Chester French and supervised the cutting of French's marble figures for the Boston Custom House in a quarry in Vermont before sailing for Paris in 1887 to study figure sculpture with Antonin Mercié and animal sculpture with Emmanuel Fremiet. He exhibited at the Salon of 1889 and returned to the United States in 1891, establishing a studio in Enfield, Massachusetts, and renewing his working relationship with French, who was recognized as the "Dean of American Sculpture" after the death of Augustus Saint-Gaudens in 1907.

French employed Potter to make the horses for six of his equestrian monument commissions (*General Grant,* Philadelphia, 1899; *General Hooker,* Boston State House lawn, 1903; *General Devens,* Worchester, Massachusetts, 1906; one of George Washington that the Daughters of the American Revolution donated to France in 1900; and two prominent groups for the World's Columbian Exposition, Chicago, 1893). Potter also created a four-horse quadriga for the Columbian Exposition, and equestrian monuments to General McClellan on the *Smith Memorial,* Philadelphia (1897–1912); General Custer, Monroe, Michigan (1910); General Kearney, Washington, D.C. (1914); Hernando DeSoto for the St. Louis Exposition (1904); and General Slocum, Gettysburg (1902). Lorado Taft wrote that there was "no more impressive sculpture upon the famous battlefield" than Potter's *Slocum.* Potter was the best animal sculptor of his day. Adeline Adams said that "no one but Edward Potter has ever told in sculpture . . . so much of the honest truth about horses" (Adams 1929, 95).

Potter was prolific. He exhibited at the Buffalo Exposition (1901) and won a medal at St. Louis (1904). He made statuary for the Library of Congress, the Brooklyn Museum, and the New York Appellate Court Building, as well as monumental portrait figures for Lansing, Michigan, and Greenwich, Connecticut. His noble lions, known colloquially as *Patience* and *Fortitude,* flanking the entrance to the New York Public Library, are among the most loved statues in New York.

References: Adams 1929; Bach and Gray 1983; Carpenter 1982; Gayle and Cohen 1988; Gurney 1985; Reynolds 1988; Riedy 1981; Small 1982.

Quinn, Edmond T. (1868–1929), 1 statue, 1 bust

Quinn was born in Philadelphia. He studied at the Pennsylvania Academy of Fine Arts and in Paris. Quinn won a silver medal at the San Francisco Exposition (1915). He was a member of the National Sculpture Society, the Architectural League of New York, the National Institute of Arts and Letters, and an associate of the National Academy of Design.

His *Edwin Booth as Hamlet* stands in New York City's Gramercy Park and his *Zoroaster* adorns the Brooklyn Museum. His monument to the

Revolutionary War battle of King's Mountain stands on the battlefield in South Carolina, and a statue of John Howard is in Williamsport, Pennsylvania. He made portrait busts for the Hall of Fame at New York University, and a small *Nymph* is in the collection of the Metropolitan Museum of Art.

References: Adams 1929; Gayle and Cohen 1988; National Sculpture Society 1929; Reynolds 1988.

Rieker, Albert George (1890–1959), 1 bust

Little is known about Rieker, who made the bust of Mississippi's Col. William Withers that was cast by Roman Bronze Works. Rieker also made a bust of Huey Pierce Long, Ogden Museum of American Art, New Orleans, Louisiana (1940); two multi-figure relief groups as a war memorial for the War Memorial Building, Jackson, Mississippi (1941); and a bronze relief portrait of E. W. Mente as the centerpiece of an exedral monument to Mente at the Touro Infirmary, New Orleans, Louisiana (1925). The *Mente Memorial* was fabricated by Albert Weiblen Marble and Granite Works, with whom Rieker was associated as an architect and designer in the 1920s.

References: Albert Weiblen Co. Papers; Roman Bronze Works Archives.

Roman Bronze Works, New York, New York

Roman Bronze Works was established in 1900 by Riccardo Bertelli, an Italian immigrant who brought his knowledge of lost-wax casting to New York in 1895. Through the 1960s, Roman Bronze Works specialized in lost-wax casting, making sculpture for many prominent figurative sculptors, including Frederic Remington, who made Roman Bronze his exclusive foundry. Between 1912 and 1922, Roman Bronze Works cast Henry Merwin Shrady's mammoth *General Grant Memorial,* Washington, D.C., the largest bronze monument of its day. In 1928, Roman Bronze Works was purchased by General Bronze Corporation, and it soon moved to the old Tiffany bronze foundry in Corona, New York, where it continued fine-arts casting and also made architectural elements such as lamps and sconces. In 1948, members of the Schiavo family, long-time employees of the company, purchased it, moved it from Corona, and operated it another three decades. Major castings include Augustus Saint-Gaudens, *Seated Lincoln,* Chicago; Daniel Chester French, *Seated Emerson,* Harvard University.

References: Roman Bronze Works Archives; Shapiro 1985.

Ross, Albert Randolph (1868–1948), *Pennsylvania Monument* and architectural services for Weinman's *Colonel Vilas Monument*

Ross was the son of an architect. He was born in Westfield, Massachusetts, grew up in Davenport, Iowa, and worked in his father's office there before moving to Buffalo, New York, and then to New York City, where he worked with McKim, Mead and White from 1891 to 1897. Ackerman and Ross operated 1898 to 1901, when Ross married and moved to Negro Island, near Boothbay Harbor, Maine, where he lived and worked for the rest of his life.

Ross designed the *Union Soldiers and Sailors Monument* in Baltimore (1909), with a heroic-scale figure group by A. A. Weinman. He also designed a dozen libraries, including those in Atlanta (1902); San Diego (1903); Nashville (1917); Denver; and Columbus, Ohio; plus the Carnegie Library in Washington, D.C. (1903); and courthouses in Milwaukee, Wisconsin, and Elizabeth, New Jersey. He was a member of the Architectural League and the National Sculpture Society.

References: Archives VNMP; Inventory of American Sculpture.

Saville, Bruce W. (1893–1938), 3 reliefs

Saville studied at the Boston Normal Art School under Cyrus Dallin, a sculptor whose best-known monumental statuary is the *Appeal to the Great Spirit,* an equestrian Native American chief outside the entrance to the Museum of Fine Arts, Boston. Saville also studied at that museum's school, and he worked in the studio of Theo and Henry Kitson for four years. He taught at Ohio State University and the Columbus Art School from 1921 to 1925. His works include the *John Hancock Monument,* Quincy, Massachusetts; *Anthony Wayne Monument,* Toledo, Ohio; *Canadian Infantryman Monument,* St. Johns, Newfoundland; war memorials in Palmyra, Maine; Westfield, Massachusetts; Chicopee, Massachusetts; and Ravenna, Ohio; and the state capitol in Columbus, Ohio. He also made the *Victory and Peace Monument,* Glen Falls, New York. Saville was a member of the National Sculpture Society, the Architectural League of New York, and the American Federation of Arts.

Reference: National Sculpture Society 1929.

Schaaf, Anton (1869–1943), 1 statue, 7 busts, 4 reliefs

Schaaf was born in Wisconsin. He studied with Kenyon Cox and Augustus Saint-Gaudens, also matriculating at the Cooper Union and the National Academy of Design under J. Q. A. Ward. He was a member of the National Sculpture Society and the Architectural League of New York. He created numerous funerary monuments and war memorials, many of which were sited in and around New York City.

References: National Sculpture Society 1929; Reynolds 1988.

Sessums, J. Kim (born 1958), *First and Third Mississippi Regiments, African Descent*

Sessums is a physician and artist who lives in Brookhaven, Mississippi. Since the 1990s, he has made several statuettes and portrait busts as well as two-dimensional art.

Reference: Ellis 2001.

Sievers, Frederick William (1872–1966), *General Tilghman* equestrian statue

Sievers was born in Fort Wayne, Indiana, and grew up in Atlanta, Georgia, and Richmond, Virginia. He studied at the Mechanics' Industrial Institute, then traveled to Rome for study at the Royal Academy of Fine Arts (1899–1901), and on to the Academy Julian in Paris. He opened a studio in New York; won the commission for the *Virginia Monument* at Gettysburg (ded. 1917); and then moved to Richmond, where he kept his studio for the rest of his life. His equestrian *Stonewall Jackson Monument* (1919) and *Matthew Fontaine Maury Monument* (1929) are prominently sited on Richmond's Monument Avenue. He also commemorated Virginia Confederates with statuary in Abingdon (1907), Leesburg (1908), Louisa (1905), and Pulaski (1906), and he made a memorial to Confederate POWs who are buried in Elmira, New York (1937). His portraits of William "Extra Billy" Smith (1906), James Madison (1931), Zachary Taylor (1931), Patrick Henry (1932), and Sam Houston are at the Virginia State Capitol.

References: Craven 1984; Craven 1982; Przybylek 1996.

Taft, Lorado (1860–1936), 1 statue on *U.S. Navy Monument*

Taft was born in Elmwood, Illinois. He studied at the University of Illinois and trained in Paris at the École des Beaux-Arts under Augustin-Alexandre Dumont, Jean-Marie-Bienaimé Bonnaissieux, and Jules Thomas between 1880 and 1885. In 1886 he joined the faculty of the Art Institute of Chicago, later teaching also at the University of Chicago.

In 1891, Taft received the sculpture commission for William Le Baron Jenny's Horticultural Building at the Columbian Exposition (1893), and he subsequently supervised fabrication of the extensive sculptural program for the temporary "White City" (1893). Multiple monumental figure groups and extensive architectural ornamentation of the Beaux Arts buildings were made using staff, a mixture of plaster of Paris and straw or hemp fiber. Among the scores of sculptors under his direction were a group of talented female artists known as the "white rabbits" because they were constantly bustling around the studios and were covered in plaster dust.

Taft won medals at the Columbian Exposition and at the expositions in Buffalo (1901), St. Louis (1904), and San Francisco (1915); also the Montgomery Ward Prize at the Art Institute of Chicago (1906). His major works include the colossal *Black Hawk,* Oregon, Illinois (1911); *Columbus Memorial Fountain* outside Union Station, Washington, D.C. (1912); *Ferguson Fountain of the Great Lakes,* Chicago (1913); *Fountain of Time,* Chicago

(1922); *Alma Mater,* Urbana, Illinois (1929); as well as fountains for Denver, Colorado, and Paducah, Kentucky, and a soldiers monument for Danville, Illinois. His *Defense of the Flag* was dedicated at Chickamauga and Chattanooga National Military Park (1895), and replicas were erected in Jackson, Michigan (1904); Marion, Indiana (1913); and Gloversville, New York (1918). He also made the relief sculptures for stone monuments to the Third and Fourth Michigan regiments at Gettysburg (1889).

Taft was a key figure in the Chicago cultural community and a great advocate for public art and civic beautification in the Midwest and beyond. He was a prolific author and speaker, writing numerous essays for newspapers and magazines, as well as *The History of American Sculpture* (1903, revised and expanded 1924 and 1930), the first comprehensive study of the subject. Taft also presented popular public lectures in which he modeled a bust of a beautiful maiden and then transformed her into an old hag before the audience. In 1907 he opened Midway Studios and operated it as a traditional atelier, training numerous young sculptors who assisted him and then went on to independent careers. He was a member of several prominent social clubs in Chicago, the National Sculpture Society, the American Academy of Arts and Letters, and he was an academician of the National Academy of Design.

References: Bach 1992; Bach and Gray 1983; Garvey 1988; Gurney 1985; Hendry 1980; National Sculpture Society 1929; Riedy 1981; Weller 1985.

Theard, Alfred F. (unknown), *Louisiana Monument*

Theard is identified as the architect for the *Louisiana Monument* on a blueprint for the monument in the Albert Weiblen Marble and Granite Company Office Papers (folder 35).

Reference: Albert Weiblen Papers.

Thomas, Steffen (1906–1990), *Alabama Monument, Colonel Forney*

Steffen Wolfgang George Thomas was born in Furth, Germany. He apprenticed with a woodcarver and studied at the School of Applied Arts in Nuremberg and the Academy of Fine Arts in Munich. He immigrated to the United States and settled in Atlanta in 1929. During his long and productive career, Thomas made paintings and sculptures and taught art. His style ranged through realism, expressionism, and abstraction.

Major works include *Atlanta Pioneer Women Memorial,* Atlanta (1938); statue of Georgia governor Eugene Talmadge and busts of Moina Bell Michael (1937) and John M. Slaton (ca. 1958) at the Georgia State Capitol; portraits of Alabama governor Bibb Graves and presidents of the universities of Alabama, George Denny, and Georgia, Steadman Sanford; also George Washington Carver for Tuskegee Institute. A museum devoted to his life and work is in Buckhead, Georgia, outside Atlanta.

References: Aiches and Janson 1997; Thomas 1951.

Tiffany Studios, New York, New York

There is an extensive bibliography on the various glass and decorating companies of Louis Comfort Tiffany (1848–1933), son of the jeweler, Charles Lewis Tiffany (1812–1902), but little published information about the bronze foundry that the younger Tiffany operated in Corona, New York, from as early as 1894 until the foundry went bankrupt in 1932. It primarily produced ecclesiastical bronzes such as lecterns and altar furnishings, but also cast portrait and allegorical statuary for fountains as well as cemetery and civic memorials.

Major castings include William Sievers's *Virginia Monument,* Gettysburg (installed 1913); a copy of Henry Kirk Bush-Brown's equestrian *George Washington* for the U.S. Military Academy, West Point, New York (1916); Belle Kinney's *Women of the Confederacy Monument,* Jackson, Mississippi (1917); firemen memorials in Walden and Newburg, New York (both 1909); and flagpole bases for the New York Public Library (1912).

Reference: Kulpa 2008.

Triebel, Frederick (1865–1944), *Mississippi Monument*

Triebel was born in Peoria, Illinois; studied in Florence; and debuted at the Columbian Exposition with small marble sculptures. He had a studio in Macdougal Alley, New York City, but also worked in Italy at times. He was the only designer of Civil War battlefield monuments other than the Muldoon Monument Company to use foreign foundries. The material composition and structural integrity of the monumental bronze eagle finial cast in Italy for his *Iowa Monument* at Shiloh National Military Park (1906) became the subject of a critical War Department investigation when it was damaged by lightning in 1909. Triebel produced a military monument, portraits of Gen. John Logan and Robert Ingersoll, and other statuary for Peoria.

References: Panhorst 1988; Taft 1924.

Van Amringe, William B. (1850–1925), *Minnesota Monument*

Van Amringe got his start as a salesman for Smith Granite Company, Westerly, Rhode Island, by 1885. While at Smith, Van Amringe was responsible for all of their war monuments. He was well-respected by other monument manufacturers, by state monument commissioners, and by the War Department's battlefield park commissioners. In 1899, he bought the equipment of Smith Granite Company's Boston office and founded his own firm, one which appears to have been atypical of the trade but still highly successful. Van Amringe specialized solely in brokering memorial art and architecture. He kept only a small office staff. Once he secured a commission he contracted with other companies to quarry, shape, and assemble the stone and to model and cast the bronze. The company also specialized in assembling monuments manufactured by others.

Reference: Panhorst 1988.

Weiblen Marble and Granite Works, *Louisiana* and *North Carolina monuments*

The firm of Albert Weiblen (1857–1957) brokered, produced, and installed monuments and memorials around the Deep South from its founding in New Orleans ca. 1888 to 1971. It specialized in making funerary monuments and mausolea with materials from company quarries. Metairie Cemetery in New Orleans is full of Weiblen memorials. Weiblen also worked dimension stone for buildings.

Weiblen was a German immigrant stone worker who arrived in New Orleans knowing his trade and rapidly built one of the largest stone companies in the South, operating a modern steam-powered plant that finished stone shipped from company quarries and other suppliers. Sons Frederick, George, and John participated in the business, as did John's wife Norma, who eventually assumed the presidency of the company after the deaths of Albert and John. John and Norma purchased Metairie Cemetery and operated it until Stewart Enterprises acquired the Weiblen holdings in 1969 and changed the company name in 1971.

A Georgia subsidiary, Stone Mountain Granite Corporation, which operated on land leased from Sam Venable, produced massive quantities of stone for monuments and buildings from 1911 to 1934. In 1936, Weiblen established another quarry at Elberton City, Georgia. The *Thomas Jefferson Memorial,* Washington, D.C. (1943), was built with "Weiblen Grey" from that quarry. Weiblen soon moved most of its manufacturing operations to the Elberton City quarry site. Weiblen was also involved in construction of the mammoth Confederate memorial relief carving on the face of Stone Mountain (1915–1970).

In 1927, Weiblen built the three-tiered *Bloom Fountain* with granite basins surmounted by a bronze allegorical figure on Crawford Street in Vicksburg. Other notable works include the *Thomas Wood Lee Monument,* City Cemetery, Monroe, Louisiana (1898); Eli Harvey's *Elks Monument,* New Orleans (1904); Edward Valentine's *Jefferson Davis Monument,* New Orleans (1911); Alexander Doyle's equestrian *General Beauregard Monument,* New Orleans (1915); and Theo Kitson's *Hiker,* New Orleans (1939).

Reference: Albert Weiblen Marble and Granite Company Records.

Weinman, Adolph Alexander (1870–1952), *Colonel Vilas Monument,* 1 relief

Weinman was born in Karlsruhe, Germany, and immigrated to New York City at age ten with his widowed mother. Apprenticed to a carver of wood and ivory at fifteen, he also studied at Cooper Union and the Art Students League. He assisted Philip Martiny, Olin Warner, Charles Niehaus, Augustus Saint-Gaudens, and Daniel Chester French, amassing considerable skill and experience with sculpture in all its forms—decorative, architectural, monumental, medallic, and portrait, in relief and in the round—before opening his own studio in 1904.

Weinman won medals at the expositions in Buffalo (1901); St. Louis (1904); and Brussels, Belgium (1910). He produced a large sculptural group, *The Destiny of the Red Man,* for the St. Louis Exposition (1904), followed by the *Maryland Union Soldiers and Sailors Monument* in Baltimore (1909), monumental statues of General Macomb (Detroit, 1908), Alexander Cassatt (Penn Station, New York, 1910), and two of Abraham Lincoln for Kentucky (Hodgenville, 1909; Frankfort, 1911). He also executed a prodigious amount of handsome Beaux Arts style architectural sculpture, including doors for the Library of Congress (1897), panels for the Morgan Library (1903–6), pediments for the National Archives (Pennsylvania Ave. side, 1933–35), capitols in Wisconsin (1911) and Missouri (1921–27), sphinxes for the Scottish Rite Temple in Washington (1915), the façade of the New York City Municipal Building (1907–14), and bronze doors for the American Academy of Arts and Letters (1938).

The Architectural League of New York awarded him a gold medal in 1913. In 1920, the American Numismatic Society honored him with the Saltus Award Medal (which he had designed in 1919). He also designed the *Mercury* dime and the *Walking Liberty* half-dollar (1916). He served as president of the National Sculpture Society (1928–31) and was a member of the National Commission of Fine Arts (1928–32).

References: Adams 1929; Bach and Gray 1983; Gayle and Cohen 1988; Gurney 1985; Hendry 1980; National Sculpture Society 1929; Proske 1943; Reynolds 1988; Riedy 1981.

Weston Studio Foundry, Santa Fe, New Mexico, casting of bronze group on *First and Third Mississippi, African Descent Monument*

This small fine arts foundry was established in 1968 and closed in 2011.
Reference: Archives VNMP.

Zabriskie, A. J.

Zabriskie, an engineer, was the secretary of the New York State Monuments Commission at the turn of the twentieth century. He supervised the design and construction of numerous monuments to New York units and individuals on several Civil War battlefields.
Reference: Panhorst 1988.

Bibliography

Unpublished Sources

Adolph Alexander Weinman Papers. Archives of American Art, Smithsonian Institution.

Albert Weiblen Marble and Granite Company Office Records. Southeastern Architectural Archive, Special Collections Division, Tulane University Libraries, New Orleans, Louisiana.

Archives, Vicksburg National Military Park. Vicksburg, Mississippi.

Frederick William Sievers Papers. The Library of Virginia, Richmond, Virginia.

Henry Hudson and Theo Alice Ruggles Kitson papers, [187-]-1979. Archives of American Art, Smithsonian Institution.

Kitson Papers. New-York Historical Society, New York.

Panhorst, Michael W. 1988. "Lest We Forget: Monuments and Memorial Sculptures on Civil War Battlefields in National Military Parks, 1861–1917." Ph.D. Dissertation. University of Delaware.

Przybylek, Leslie A. 1996. "Soldiers to Science: Changing Commemorative Ideals in the Public Sculpture of Frederick William Sievers." M.A. Thesis. University of Delaware.

Roman Bronze Works Archives. Amon Carter Museum of American Art, Ft. Worth, Texas.

Tiffany Studios. Bronze Work. New York: Tiffany Studios, ca. 1912. (Album of photographs in the Prints & Drawings Collection, Metropolitan Museum of Art, New York.)

Published Sources

Abernathy, Alonzo (compiler). 1908. *Dedication of Monuments Erected by the State of Iowa Commemorating the Death, Suffering, and Valor of Her Soldiers on the Battlefields of Vicksburg, Lookout Mountain, Missionary Ridge, Shiloh, and in the Confederate Prison at Andersonville.* Des Moines: Emory H. English, State Printer and E. D. Chassell, State Binder.

Adams, Adeline. 1929. *The Spirit of American Sculpture.* New York: National Sculpture Society.

Aiches, Alan Z., and Anthony F. Janson. 1997. *The Art of Steffen Thomas.* Buckhead, GA: Steffen Thomas Museum and Archives.

Ames, David, and Michael W. Panhorst. 1985. "Preliminary Estimate of the Effects of Environmental Factors on the Corrosion of Monumental Bronze Statue Replicas Erected in Different Locations in the Northeastern United States."

Newark, Delaware: Published in report form for the National Park Service, Preservation Assistance Division, by the Center for Historic Architecture and Engineering, University of Delaware.

Bach, Ira J., and Mary Lackritz Gray. 1983. *A Guide to Chicago's Public Sculpture.* Chicago: University of Chicago Press.

Bach, Penny Balkin. 1992. *Public Art in Philadelphia.* Philadelphia: Temple University Press.

Birnbaum, Charles, and Robin S. Karson. 2000. *Pioneers of American Landscape Design.* New York: McGraw-Hill.

Caffin, Charles H. 1913. *American Masters of Sculpture.* New York: Doubleday, Page.

Carpenter, Charles H., Jr. 1982. *Gorham Silver: 1831–1981.* New York: Dodd, Mead.

Cocke, Edward J. 1968. *Monumental New Orleans.* New Orleans: La Fayette.

Couper, Greta Elena. 1988. *An American Sculptor on the Grand Tour.* Los Angeles, CA: TreCavalli Press.

Craven, Wayne. 1984. *Sculpture in America.* Newark, DE: University of Delaware Press.

———. 1982. *The Sculptures at Gettysburg.* Gettysburg, PA: Eastern Acorn Press.

Ellis, Jennifer. 2001. "Portrait of an Artist . . . or Two," *Mississippi Magazine,* Jan./Feb.: 31–34, 82–83.

Evert, Marilyn. 1983. *Discovering Pittsburgh's Sculpture.* Pittsburgh: University of Pittsburgh Press.

Garvey, Timothy J. 1988. *Public Sculptor: Lorado Taft and the Beautification of Chicago.* Urbana: University of Illinois.

Gault, William P. 1906. *Ohio At Vicksburg. Report of the Ohio Vicksburg Battlefield Commission.* Columbus: Vicksburg Battlefield Commission.

Gayle, Margot, and Michele Cohen. 1988. *Guide to Manhattan's Outdoor Sculpture.* New York: Prentice Hall.

Goode, James. 1974. *Outdoor Sculpture of Washington, D.C.: A Comprehensive Guide.* Washington, DC: Smithsonian Institution Press.

Greenthal, Katherine, P. M. Kozol, and J. S. Ramirez. 1986. *American Figurative Sculpture in the Museum of Fine Arts, Boston.* Boston: Museum of Fine Arts, Boston.

Gurney, George. 1985. *Sculpture and the Federal Triangle.* Washington, DC: Smithsonian Institution Press.

Hendry, Fay L. 1980. *Outdoor Sculpture of Grand Rapids.* Okemos, MI: Iota.

Hills, Parker. 2012. *Vicksburg National Military Park: Art of Commemoration.* Vicksburg: Vicksburg Convention and Visitors Bureau.

Illinois-Vicksburg Military Park Commission. 1907. *Illinois at Vicksburg.* Chicago: Blakely Printing.

Isbell, Timothy. 2006. *Vicksburg: Sentinels of Stone.* Jackson: University Press of Mississippi.

Keller, Martha R., and Michael J. Curtis. 1995. *Public Art in Ann Arbor and Washtenaw County.* Ann Arbor: Alexa Lee Gallery.

Kozar, Andrew J. 1975. *R. Tait McKenzie: The Sculptor of Athletes.* Knoxville: University of Tennessee Press.

Lee, Ronald F. 1973. *The Origin and Evolution of the National Military Park Idea.* Washington, DC: National Park Service.

Little, Carol. 1996. *A Comprehensive Guide to Outdoor Sculpture in Texas.* Austin: University of Texas Press.

Marks, Barbara, ed. 2000. *Flesh and Stone: Stony Creek and the Age of Granite.* Stony Creek, CT: Stony Creek Granite Quarry Workers Celebration.

McDougal, Isabel. 1908. "Leonard Crunelle, Sculptor of Children," *Craftsman* 15, Oct.: 32.

Minnesota-Vicksburg Monument Commission. 1907. *Report of the Minnesota-Vicksburg Monument Commission to the Governor of Minnesota.* Minnesota: n.p.

National Sculpture Society. 1929. *Contemporary American Sculpture,* exh. cat., The California Palace of the Legion of Honor. New York: Kalkhoff.

Naude, Virginia Norton, ed. 1985. *Sculptural Monuments in an Outdoor Environment.* Philadelphia: Pennsylvania Academy of the Fine Arts.

Panhorst, Michael W. 1999. "Herbert Adams" in John Garraty and Mark Carnes, eds. *American National Biography.* New York: Oxford University Press.

——. 2014. "'The First of Our Hundred Battle Monuments,' Civil War Battlefield Monuments Built by Active-Duty Soldiers during the Civil War," *Southern Cultures* 20, no. 4: 22–43.

Proske, Beatrice Gilman. 1943. *Brookgreen Gardens Sculpture,* vol. 1. Murrells Inlet, SC: Brookgreen Gardens.

——. 1955. *Brookgreen Gardens Sculpture,* vol. 2. Murrells Inlet, SC: Brookgreen Gardens.

Reynolds, Donald Martin. 1988. *Monuments and Masterpieces: Histories and Views of Public Sculpture in New York City.* New York: Macmillan.

Rhode Island Vicksburg Monument Commission. 1909. *Report of Rhode Island Vicksburg Monument Commission to the General Assembly.* Providence: Snow and Farnham.

Riedy, James. 1981. *Chicago Sculpture.* Urbana: University of Illinois Press.

Rubenstein, Charlotte Streifer. 1990. *American Women Sculptors.* Boston: G. K. Hall.

Salmon, Robin R. 1993. *Brookgreen Gardens Sculpture,* vol. 2. Murrells Inlet, SC: Brookgreen Gardens.

Savage, Kirk. 1997. *Standing Soldiers, Kneeling Slaves: Race, War, and Monument in Nineteenth-Century America.* Princeton: Princeton University Press.

Sellars, Richard West. 2005. *Pilgrim Places: Civil War Battlefields, Historic Preservation, and America's First National Military Parks, 1893–1900.* Ft. Washington, PA: Eastern National.

Shapiro, Michael. 1985. *Bronze Casting and American Sculpture, 1850–1900.* Newark: University of Delaware Press.

Sloan, Katharine A., and Helen S. Schwartz. 2008. *Vicksburg: A Photographic Journey with Voices from the Past.* Langhorne, PA: Artistry in Photography.

Small, Herbert. 1982. *The Library of Congress: Its Architecture and Decoration.* New York: W. W. Norton.

Smith, Timothy B. 2008. *The Golden Age of Civil War Battlefield Preservation: The Decade of the 1890s and the Establishment of America's First Five Military Parks.* Knoxville: University of Tennessee Press.

——. 2009. *A Chickamauga Memorial: The Establishment of America's First Civil War National Military Park.* Knoxville: University of Tennessee Press.

Society of Medalists. 1967. *Seventy-Fifth Issue, Herring Coe, Sculptor.* New York: Society of Medalists.

Taft, Lorado. 1924. *History of American Sculpture.* New York: Macmillan.

Thomas, Steffen. 1951. *Sculpture by Steffen Thomas*. Stone Mountain, GA: Steffen Thomas Studio.

Turak, Theodore. 1986. *William Le Baron Jenney: A Pioneer of Modern Architecture*. Architecture and Urban Design 17. Ann Arbor, MI: UMI Research Press.

U.S. Department of the Interior. 2000. National Park Service. "Highways in Harmony: Vicksburg National Military Park Tour Roads," brochure published by the Historic American Engineering Record.

Walker, Steve, David Riggs, and Harold Young. 1984. *Vicksburg Battlefield Monuments: A Pictorial Record*. Jackson: University Press of Mississippi.

Wasserman, Jean, ed. 1975. *Metamorphoses in Nineteenth-Century Sculpture*. Cambridge, MA: Fogg Art Museum and Harvard University Press.

Weller, Allen Stuart. 1985. *Lorado in Paris: The Letters of Lorado Taft, 1880–1885*. Urbana: University of Illinois Press.

Online Sources

Catalog of American Portraits. Smithsonian Institution. npgportraits.si.edu

Inventory of American Sculpture, Smithsonian Institution. www.siris.si.edu

The Making of The Poet: Lord Byron video shows the process of making a monumental bronze sculpture with sand molds in 1999 at marshallfredericks.org/learn

For information about A.R.T. Enterprises see www.thinksculpture.com

For information about Gary Casteel see www.garycasteel.com

For information about the Hughes Granite and Marble Company see www.sandusky-county-scrapbook.net/Hughes.htm

For Modern Art Foundry see http://www.modernartfoundry.com/about.html

For video of the dedication of the Ninth Connecticut Monument see www.jimlarkin.com/9thRegiment/9thRegimentHome.htm and for information about its design and fabrication see www.casualclicks.com

Kulpa, Paula Kristina. "An Investigation into Louis Comfort Tiffany's and Tiffany Studios' Architectural Metalwork." M.A. Thesis. University of Pennsylvania, 2008. http://repository.upenn.edu/cgi/viewcontent.cgi?article=1111&context=hp_theses

Index

Adams, Daniel W. (Brig. Gen.), 13, 124
Adams, Herbert, 43, 49, 76, 119, 135, 158
Adams, John (Brig. Gen.), 122
African Descent, First and Third Mississippi Regiments, Monument. *See* Mississippi, First and Third Regiments, African Descent, Monument
Alabama Monument, 27–33, 36, 47, 51, 58, 71, 105, 125, 147, 153
Alexander, Jesse I. (Col.), 118
American Bronze Company, American Bronze Foundry Company, American Art Bronze, 21, 52, 119, 121–22, 126, 136, 140
Anderson, Joseph W. (Maj.), 128
Arkansas Monument, 22, 24, 72, 96, 124
A.R.T. Research Enterprises, 52, 136, 160

Baldwin, William E. (Brig. Gen.), 123
Barton, Seth M. (Brig. Gen.), 129
Benton, William P. (Brig. Gen.), 127
Berchem, Jules, 54, 118, 122–24, 126–29, 136, 140
Blair, Francis P., Jr. (Maj. Gen.), 120
Boomer, George B. (Col.), 118
Borglum, Solon H., 45, 49, 120, 123, 125, 127, 130, 137
Bowen, John S. (Maj. Gen.), 123
Breckinridge, John C. (Maj. Gen.), 126
Brenholtz, Thomas S. (Lt. Col.), 121
Brewster, George T., 45, 49, 119–20, 123–26, 128–30, 137
Bryant, George E. (Col.), 72, 128
Buckland, Ralph P. (Brig. Gen.), 121
Buford, Abraham (Brig. Gen.), 129
Burbridge, Stephen G. (Brig. Gen.), 118
Bureau Brothers, 52–53, 108, 123, 137, 158
Bussy, Cyrus (Col.), 120

Campbell, Robert (Maj.), 125
Carr, Eugene A. (Brig. Gen.), 127
Casteel, Gary, 47, 49, 107, 126, 136–38
Chambers, Alexander (Col.), 120
Cianfarani, Aristide Berto, 49, 120, 128, 138
Cockerill, Joseph R. (Col.), 120
Cockrell, Francis M. (Col.), 123
Coe, Herring, 24, 49, 103, 125, 138, 159

Columbian Exposition, 2, 8, 44, 84, 132–33, 135, 140, 143–44, 147–48, 152, 154
Comstock, Cyrus B. (Capt.), 120
Confederate Dead, Monument to the. *See* Monument to the Confederate Dead
Connecticut Monument, 14, 39, 41, 72, 117, 130, 160
Cosby, George B. (Brig. Gen.), 126
Couper, William, 22, 44, 49, 66, 75, 90, 118–20, 122, 125, 139
Cottrell, W. Liance, 19, 43, 50, 79, 119, 139
Crocker, Marcellus M. (Brig. Gen.), 119
Crunelle, Leonard, 44, 49, 78, 119, 140, 159
Cumming, Alfred (Brig. Gen.), 72, 128
Curtin, Andrew G. (Gov.), 121
Curtin, John I. (Col.), 121

Davis, Charles Henry (Flag Officer), 72, 90, 122
Davis, Jefferson (Pres.), 11, 25, 30
Davis, Jefferson (Pres.), Monument, 25, 68, 102, 125
Davis, Jefferson (Pres.), portrait figure on *Kentucky Monument,* 30, 45, 47, 71, 107, 126, 136
Dennis, Elias S. (Brig. Gen.), 120
Dockery, Thomas P. (Col.), 124
Durell, George W. (Capt.), 121

Ector, Matthew D. (Brig. Gen.), 127
Ellet, Alfred W. (Brig. Gen.), 122
Elwell, Francis Edwin, 45, 49, 82, 90, 120–23, 127, 140
Engleman, Adolph (Col.), 122
Erwin, Eugene (Col.), 119
Evans, Nathan G. (Brig. Gen.), 129
Ewing, Hugh (Brig. Gen.), 120

Farragut, David (Adm.), 45, 68, 72, 90, 122
Farrar, Bernard G. (Col.), 122
Featherston, Winfield S. (Brig. Gen.), 129
Ferrero, Edward (Brig. Gen.), 120
First and Third Mississippi Regiments, African Descent, Monument, 47, 51, 72, 81, 120, 152, 156
Florentine Brotherhood Foundry, 52, 121, 136, 140